Walking Thinking Drinking Across Scotland

Walking, Thinking, Drinking Across Scotland

One man's search for joy - or at least a Guinness

by Tom Trimbath

Walking, Thinking, Drinking Across Scotland
One man's search for joy - or at least a Guinness

Other books by Tom (T. E.) Trimbath

Just Keep Pedaling
Twelve Months at Barclay Lake
Twelve Months at Lake Valhalla
Twelve Months at Merritt Lake
Dream. Invest. Live.

Table of Contents

Breaking Out of a Rut

September 21
Seattle - Glasgow

Sunny beaches? Ha! I was headed to misty Scotland for my autumn vacation. What was I thinking? My friends wondered about that too. So did I, but I trust my intuition. I knew I needed a change of scenery and a different routine.

We build ruts. We build them out of habits and for a purpose, even if we don't realize it. Our ruts keep us in the vicinity of what we think we need and aim us towards a goal we expect to reach. A rut is a person's self-built one-dimensional maze that includes walls and a picture of cheese. If it is a deep enough rut the horizon becomes the top of the trench that we can't see over. The world shrinks to something that seems controllable where everything except the end is within reach. We humans are very good at putting ourselves into silly situations.

I knew I was in a rut, and that my horizons to either side had become a bit too near. I'd been there before, and I'd found a way out of it. I had to do something completely different. My desire to walk across Scotland was a desire to see my rut from another perspective, even if it meant creating a new rut. I did something similar ten years earlier, but that time I was just trying to lose weight.

For eight weeks in September and October of 2000 I bicycled from Washington State to Florida: a corner-to-corner bicycle ride partly intended as weight reduction, partly to get out of the house, partly to see if I could. Surely over three thousand miles of low-impact aerobics, called bicycling, would finally shift my body to a new set point and weight.

Every morning I got up early enough that by noon I'd ridden past that sunrise's horizon. Even in the petroleum-based land of America, my bicycle carried me beyond most people's borders within an hour. Ten miles down the road and I'd see places the morning's motel clerk hadn't visited in years unless their second job or Wal-Mart was there. Every day was different, but every day was the same. Despite being on a transcontinental adventure and crossing every type of terrain, I'd simply traded one rut for another. Most of the habits were logistical: wake up, pack up, ride for hours, get tired, find a room, find food, get some sleep, repeat. My life in suburbia had its own set of habits: mow the lawn, wash the windows, pull the weeds, etc., etc. Ruts are everywhere.

Somewhere along the ride I realized that my ruts weren't built from comfort zones. My ruts were dug by shoulds. Each day I felt that I should make progress, I should lose weight, I shouldn't frighten the locals. Lyrca wasn't welcome everywhere. Then I realized my habits back home were based on shoulds too. That wasn't how life should be.

My intent was to ride all the way to Key West, the southernmost tip of Florida and the country, but I only made it to Pensacola, in the northwest corner of the state, before I ran out of time and money. At the end of two months of bicycling I was tired, the same weight, the same waist size, the same percentage body fat, and poorer. The stock market internet implosion had begun. My timely sale of AOL had been enough to pay for the trip but the rest of the portfolio rode the drop. I'm an optimist. I hoped the downturn would only last weeks, but it went on for years. I was married then. I'd hoped to return to a celebration of the ride, my accomplishment, and a better home life. Eight weeks of low impact aerobics were supposed to be cheap, stress-reducing, and should have given my wife a skinnier husband for Christmas. My return wasn't as joyous as I'd hoped and I hadn't generated much internally either.

Despite the joy deficit I found a gem when I returned. Along the way I emailed updates to my wife so she could pass them along to friends and the curious. It saved her from repeating herself and minimized the disruption in her life. Emailing from truck stops in 2000 was a new concept and involved some of the dirtiest keyboards I'd ever seen. At least my efforts were worth it. People enjoyed the emails. For months people told me that I should write a book about my trip. That's nice. I took all of their comments as simple politeness until a writer friend cornered me and emphatically told me that they weren't just being polite. I had 15,000 words in those emails, had stories to tell, and had more than enough notes and experiences to write a book. I should shut up, listen to everyone, and write the book. So I did.

I wrote. They were right. There were stories to tell and the book filled out nicely, but something didn't feel right. Maybe that was the first sign that I was becoming a writer. I was getting picky. The story didn't gel because it felt unresolved. I felt incomplete too. I hadn't crossed the finish line: Key West. I'd started on an island in the Northwest and wanted to end on an island in the Southeast. The rest of Florida nagged at me. I resolved to ride it in the fall of 2001.

Bad timing. September 11 happened. Planes didn't fly. People didn't travel. Defenses went up. Fear and paranoia spread. Getting a bicycle and tools down to a part of the country that might not like skintight bike bibs was a discouragement.

I went anyway.

The nation was changed. We were in mourning and trying to cope with a shattered invulnerability. I'd changed too, but my changes were latent, deeply internal; but apparently something was happening. I wondered about my self and I wondered about our nation's identity while I rode through an empty Orlando. Near the end I was frustrated yet glad to be challenged by something real, natural, and apolitical: Hurricane Michelle. I made it to Key West with less than a day to spare.

Three weeks of riding through vacated vacation towns and being chased by a hurricane got me to closure.

When I reached Key West my arrival was understated and performed. I was supposed to feel celebratory but I only felt the relief of accomplishing a significant chore. I purposely shouted and threw a tired fist in the air, and quickly regrabbed the handlebars. Maybe it looked like more of a celebration to a pedestrian, but no one applauded or shook my hand. In retrospect I recall that inner voice asking, "Is this all there is?" There were no banners. No one there knew what I'd done. To them, my scene may have merely been one of a bicyclist completing a long ride from Miami, not Seattle. Nothing acknowledged my accomplishment from the outside, and nothing inside suddenly revealed itself. I'd hoped that some hidden switch would suddenly fill me with cheer, but whatever shifted hadn't surfaced.

At the time I didn't know how to step out of an emotional rut. I wasn't aware that I was shoulded into a corner. I couldn't find what I wanted: joy.

Less than a year later, the book, "Just Keep Pedaling", was done. As I say in the book, "I can't say that it was fun, but I'm glad I did it." It took me years to understand what I'd written to myself.

About ten years later much had happened. We'd passed through what one friend calls the Dismal Decade. He was talking about the nation and the planet. I lived through my own version.

My life passed through a series of powerful episodes. I got a divorce, wrote about a book a year, began selling my nature photographs, and moved to an island called Whidbey. My books, photos, talks, and advice received sweet compliments but not enough sales to pay the bills. I had a high compliment to sales quotient. My mortgage company didn't care. They sent the monthly bills regardless of my subjective accomplishments.

New friends appeared: dancers, writers, neighbors, instigators, innovative thinkers. Parties kicked in, even when they were supposed to be charitable functions. I learned that when I danced, I smiled - and realized that there was no reason to analyze that reaction.

At the suggestion of friends who were intrigued by my early retirement, I finished and self-published a book about my version of personal finance called, "Dream. Invest. Live." They liked the way I de-mystified the investing world. I had been hesitant to write it, but some of the encouragement came from authors of bestsellers. That's a hint that's hard to ignore.

But even good lives pass through stressful times; especially if bad habits or unlearned lessons persist. In other words, being human. I am human. The book's timing was atrocious. It was late 2008. The market dove again, and people worried that it was more than a market correction. The basis of our economic system was questioned. When I looked to my support network I found them looking back at me because writing the book made me look like an expert. They wanted answers because they were stressed out too. My only answer was that the upset was probably temporary, though it might take a few years; but that if it was a true collapse the only thing to do was be very flexible and adaptable. My financial life played out in public. In a very honest and open fashion, I'd described my investing life and strategy, and then was just as open and honest as my portfolio was trashed. A large aspect of my identity was publicly chastened.

Business financial stresses compounded with personal financial stresses compounded with apparent global financial failure at a time when a support network changed direction equaled an inordinate amount of stress and a lot of personal doubt. The stress showed in old-age aches and pains that were decades too early for my fifty-year-old body. Head, chest, gut, and nerve pains showed up simultaneously. There's an old, probably misquoted, Chinese proverb that says, a life well lived is marked by a body that uses up every organ all at once. It felt that way, but it didn't feel like an accomplishment. It felt more like a punishment than a life well-lived. I definitely felt mortal.

Whatever was happening was apparent to all. Walking was difficult. My energy was low. My friends knew something was wrong when I had to leave a dance after only a song or two. There were days when I could only lay on the couch and wait for the pains to subside.

Doctors made guesses and ordered expensive tests. Stress from financial woes is not eased by spending thousands more on tests that might lead to thousands more on the chance of cures. One specialist was head down, taking notes, while in my frustration I rambled and ranted about how unhealthy I felt despite diet, exercise, and lots of earnest effort. At one point I said, "Sometimes I think I'm just worrying myself sick." His response, without lifting his head or stopping his writing was, "We have a saying. Sometimes if you let the patient talk long enough they'll tell you what's really happening." His official prescription was for a colonoscopy plus another test that I also couldn't afford even with insurance. His unofficial prescription followed two questions. "Got a girlfriend?" "No." "Got a dog?" "No." "You should get one of those." He didn't specify which one. He also recommended more wine.

My friends' opinions were that I needed a vacation. They used other terms sometimes. "You should love yourself more.", "You should treat yourself better." "You should . . . " You should . . ." "You shouldn't should on yourself." But it's okay if they should on me? I got the point.

The bills from the first tests proved to me that the cost of the vacation was less than the cost of modern medicine. Doctor, I know which prescription I am going to fill first. If the underlying cause was emotional then healing my mind would be a quicker way to heal my body. I needed a vacation, even if the costs would mostly become temporary credit card debt. Everyone agreed with my prognosis and expected me to head to a sunny, sandy shore.

Eventually my portfolio recovered enough to encourage me to hope. I wanted to wait until my portfolio was overflowing, then I could afford tests and treatments, make sure nothing was biologically broken, and then take the vacation; but I didn't want to wait out another Great Depression.

I follow intuition and notice coincidence. It seemed appropriate to commemorate the tenth anniversary of a self-powered, diagonal, cross-country trek with another one. The first one took 11 weeks and $15,000. Walking across a smaller country would be simpler, shorter, and cheaper. Scotland was about the right size, and theoretically I knew the language. There might be sunny and warm countries I could walk across in less than a month, but I didn't want to take the time to learn a new language. Scottish might be tough enough.

It was time to leave. I locked myself out of my house on purpose. My trip was going to be a minimalist's journey. No computer, no cell phone, no fancy camera meant not having to worry about them or carry them. Leaving the keys at home saved very little weight, but more importantly, leaving them behind left behind the reminders of responsibilities. A friend drove me to the airport shuttle in the dark and the fog. She'd continue an early commute to her very responsible job. I'd start a very long day of traveling that would start weeks of walking.

Even as we drove to the shuttle I asked, "Why was I doing this?" I had excuses for doing it, but I also had doubts because I knew that I didn't know my core reasons. Maybe I was simply rationalizing some frivolous spending.

The rules for flying, at least as a passenger, had changed dramatically since the last time I flew off the continent. Airport security had a level of paranoia that encroached on any relaxed notion of vacation. But people adapt and tourists still tour.

The flight from Philadelphia to Glasgow was either overbooked or had plenty of room. Who and how I asked changed the answer. I was curious about the deal they'd offer me to step aside for an overbooked overseas flight. No problem. I got on.

Lucky me. The flight had to avoid a hurricane; but hurricanes are not big circles drawn from nice, sharp lines. They have splayed spiral arms that reach far beyond the main body of clouds. We dipped and bumped through waves of air while I was strapped in tight. Flight testing back at Boeing taught me to respect holes in the sky and to trust airplane integrity. The airplane is fine. The weak part is the human body. Strap it in, and don't order a drink unless it can be drunk quickly. My gin & tonic was just right for dinner, but skip the ice cubes next time. They never had a chance to do their work.

Make jokes about airline food if you want. I am proactive. The day before the flight I'd cooked up the last of the bacon and bought some fried chicken from my favorite deli. I ate when I was hungry and didn't have to wait for the pilot to release the flight attendants. Each time I unwrapped my food supply my seatmates looked over with envy or frustration. I had aromatic finger food that wouldn't spill and that didn't have to wait for the dinner cart. No. I didn't bring enough for everyone. But I did have to finish it before passing through customs and immigration.

Border guards don't like meat products coming into their country. I was compelled to enjoy bacon for breakfast and fried chicken for lunch. Ah, the happy concessions of unconventional traveling.

Sleep came in snatches across the Atlantic. Even at home, sleep and sweet dreams were uncommon. Financial woes, bodily aches, a long bout of single-ness meant I usually slept poorly. Wedged into a coach seat didn't seem like the optimum bedding, but somehow it worked. A part of me must have already made a transition. I'd already passed from dawn to dusk and was filling out immigration forms as we passed back into the edges of the penumbra and another dawn. Flying the opposite direction of the planet's spin creates lots of sunrises and loses track of days.

From Contrails To Steel Rails

September 22
Glasgow - Stranraer

  I stepped off the plane with my day-and-a-half pack stuffed with everything that I wasn't wearing and shuffled into line for whatever booth was before us. Was it immigration, customs, or passport control? It didn't matter. Answer the questions. Don't be glib. But I smiled when he raised an eyebrow at what I planned to do. He smiled back and waved me through. Welcome to Scotland.

I was a tourist with my own idea of a tour. My itinerary was short and simple. Fly into Glasgow, somehow get to Stranraer in the southwest corner, and then start walking northeast towards Dundee and maybe Aberdeen, and maybe beyond. Take a train back to Glasgow and a series of planes back to Seattle. The details were blank. My plan wasn't full of hotel reservations, train and bus schedules, or specific routes. I guessed that trains and buses would connect Stranraer, Glasgow, and Aberdeen. I trusted that I'd find sidewalks, trails, paths, or at least a tolerance for a man walking along roads. I was going to tour Scotland in a way that wasn't in any brochure. I'd checked. Of course, maybe there was a reason no one else had done what I was about to try.

So now what? I stood in Glasgow's airport without a clue about how to get to Stranraer. I needed a train or a bus, and if I couldn't find those; well, I guessed I'd skip Stranraer, start in Glasgow instead, and head towards Edinburgh. It would be coast-to-coast across the narrowest part of Scotland, and yes, I'd thought of that cheat ahead of time. If all else failed I'd make a very short trip, declare victory, and find someplace cheap and nice to hangout for a few weeks.

Off to the far right, in a tiny closet-sized kiosk was a Tourist Information booth and my first real encounter with accent and vocabulary. I started by pronouncing Stranraer so poorly that we had to pull out a map. Then I got a lesson in currencies, pounds and pence. But he was agreeable and steered me to a bus that took me to the train.

I'd hoped the train station would be connected to the airport. Nope. The train station was in downtown Glasgow, hours of walking away. I wasn't ready for that yet. I needed sleep and at least a day of recuperating from hours of jet lag. The rule of thumb is one day of recovery for every hour of jet lag. I had about a week of recovery ahead of me. So, even though it delayed the start of my walk, I jumped into the bus. As the bus pulled out from under the building, I noticed the drenching rain. It was fall. I was in Scotland. The bus was a good idea. It was much better than walking through drenching rain for hours without enough rest was a recipe for spending my vacation recovering from some bug.

As if the rain wasn't enough to convince me to ride, the roads around the airport weren't set up for pedestrians. Rush hour was a familiar packed chaos on roads with random shoulders and big puddles.

My first view of a roundabout heading clockwise relieved me of any doubts about renting a car and driving. I wondered if I would have survived the airport parking lot.

I settled in and watched Glasgow turn from airport to industrial to residential to urban. The wet windows weren't encouraging. Despite the obscured view I settled into traveler's mode. Yes, this place is different, but there's a lot of familiarity. The grass is green. The sky is wet. Traffic is packed. On the one hand I wondered why I came this far to find someplace that looked a lot like Seattle. But the familiar made me comfortable enough to be willing to adventure into the unknown.

The first major unknown was called downtown Glasgow. The bus dropped me off in cut stone canyons of busy cobblestone streets and a confusion of unfamiliar signs. Thanks to BBC reruns I was at least somewhat versed in zebra crossings and such. Somewhere in the deep maze was a train station. In Seattle the train station stands alone at the edge of downtown surrounded by parking lots and a stadium. It's obvious. To my jet-lagged American eyes, every building in Glasgow looked alike and none of them looked like something a train could pull into and out of. They even seemed to be too tightly grouped for cars. Locomotives wouldn't fit.

I knew that I'd spend the next three weeks asking stupid tourist questions and didn't see any reason to hold back. Besides, anyone I met would probably never see me again. I could be a fool amongst strangers. I asked a nicely suited gentleman for directions to the station. Hallelujah, he wasn't confused by my accent. He recognized it and apologized for the weather. I told him I was from around Seattle. That launched his great description of his love for Frazier, the sit-com set in a fictitious Seattle. While we stood there getting wet he talked about his favorite characters and lines, and threw a few sentences my way about how to find the train. Then he was off to work. At that point I knew slightly more about Glasgow than I did about a sit-com that I'd never watched.

His directions didn't make a lot of sense. It had nothing to do with his mild accent. My problem was that I couldn't see the sun to get some sense of direction. Two turns later I was lost. Why didn't the bus drop me off closer to the train station?

Well, it did and his directions were good enough. A peek into a medieval archway showed an enormous iron and glass vaulted ceiling. A few steps in and the walls swept back to become shopfronts that wrapped themselves around the terminal. Without an apology I gawked at the sudden transition and didn't start moving again until the tidal action of the crowds pulled me forward.

Refocus, dude. I wanted to gawk some more, but there were a few more things that should be done. Find the schedule. Find the ticket counter. Ask more naive questions. Find the train. Get on board. Relax for a few hours, but watch the terrain for clues about the route that might lie ahead.

The main schedule board was large and broken into columns with details of departures and arrivals. Another section showed the queue of trains that couldn't fit on the other list. It didn't make any sense. I couldn't tell if I was early or late. A station employee pointed me to the ticket counter. I wound through the empty serpentine roped line and stepped up to a wild-haired lad separated from the line of one customer by a thirty-foot long wall of glass. Evidently I was there in a lull, despite the hordes I'd seen. We barely understood each other, but he gave me a ticket and some incomprehensible directions about where to find the train. Glass walls don't aid communication.

Back in the concourse the departure board started to make sense. It looked like there were two trains to take and no clue about why they were different. At least neither was due for a while, so I had enough time to find a cash machine, get some local currency, and maybe find something to eat. My body was confused about mealtimes and I decided to just keep giving it food on a regular basis until some regularity was established, maybe about the time I got back to Seattle. Never overlook the ease with which banks can reach across borders to dole out cash. Credit cards and debit cards make traveling so much easier than starting a trip with thick wads of bills, or in the case of Scotland pockets of pounds. Food didn't translate as well. While it is easy to make a joke about Scottish cuisine, my difficulties were personal. My beleaguered condition, unfamiliar menus, and my recent diet revelation to avoid gluten (eating it seemed to cause mood crashes) meant that I bought a Scottish banana and called it breakfast.

Okay, enough of this food and cash stuff, I had to find the right train. Ask a question. Follow a sign. Ask a question. Follow a sign. Give up listening to the announcements because they just sounded like reverberating racetrack chatter. Finally walk so far to the right that I'm sure there's only wall left, and another set of tracks appear. I wandered down an empty loading area, wondering if I would be the only passenger, or if I'd gone too far, or if everyone showed up exactly on time. There was a train, an electric one, modern without being futuristic, with lots of windows, empty seats and locked doors. It felt like a storage spur and a dead end. Moments later, other people arrived. I'd asked enough questions for a while and decided to simply join the small herd that was forming farther down the platform.

They had bike racks. I could've brought my bicycle. Nah. I'd probably still be back in the airport putting it together, getting it through security, and then having to ride in the rain. Besides, my record for a one day ride is 200 miles. Crossing Scotland in a day wasn't my goal. I was on a three week vacation.

Minutes before the train was scheduled to leave we were all idly standing on the siding. Then ding, and nothing. A few seconds later the doors hadn't opened but the people moved. The ding was the sign that the doors were unlocked and that they could be opened by hitting a button. Without the crowd I would've waited for the doors to open automatically and probably would've watched an empty train pull out without me. I learned a bit by standing back and watching. The price was feeling sheepish inside.

The tired traveler wanted to sleep but the trip planner wanted to watch the terrain. The train ride would roughly parallel my most likely route. A preview of the walk was a good idea. I'd been told to expect pubs and B&Bs every mile, sidewalks and shoulders, and friendly terrain. A three week pub crawl sounded like a great vacation. Instead I saw rain. Rain that flooded fields, puddled onto roads, and drained my expectations. Scotland was rural and open and bucolic and pretty. I like that. But, I'd been told to expect density too, houses, businesses, and traveler's oases almost continually strung along the rural roads. Instead I saw farmland like back in Pennsylvania, rolling hills, roads that snaked along valley drainages, only occasional buildings, some occupied, many abandoned. Stone walls either contoured or cut across the round slopes, measuring pastures in convenient and productive parcels. Sheep and cattle vastly outnumbered people. Even most of the train stations looked empty and isolated. If the gaps between towns were too long, my walk could become either an exercise in knocking on farmhouses doors at sunset, or a series of bus rides, one town to the next, with a walking tour through the neighborhoods in the afternoons. I didn't want either of those. I wanted to walk until I was tired and then relax in comfort without imposing on anyone. The exercise should be good for me. A pub at the bottom of the stairs sounded even better.

After lunch the train pulled into the last station, Stranraer, an actual city that was much larger than I'd expected. It is also the ferry terminal for the ride to Ireland. I hadn't known that, but my house was on an island and in the town with a ferry terminal. Serendipity started me with the hint of a comfort zone. Stranraer was much bigger and the ferry much larger. One look at that parking lot and it was obviously there for fleets of cars to be carried on a longer journey. It wasn't a commuter route from a bedroom community. The ferry long enough for hundreds of cars and had sea doors instead of open decking. In a bow to serendipity and style I could've gotten a ticket to start and end my travel day on ferries.

But I wasn't going there. It was after noon. I'd been traveling for 18 hours across 8 time zones and all I wanted was a place to nap, eat, and then sleep. I'd decide what to do with my three weeks in the morning.

The painted lines directing pedestrians around the train and ferry parking lots only misled me once. Tired eyes probably missed a sign. I eventually found the main waterfront street and had no idea where to go next. Ah, the glory of totally unencumbered itineraries, moments of "Well, I guess I asked for this." Even in America, where people fight to keep the government from being useful, there are tourist information signs and booths. Scotland, part of the United Kingdom, and part of a more mature culture would surely have assistance for travelers. And they did. I saw a sign with a big "i" on it. It looked like a sanctuary to me.

Tourist information was a few blocks away. A short walk brought me to their storefront and into a room full of maps and brochures. My brain wanted that much information but was too tired to take it in.

One very understanding woman listened to my plans, smiled at my accent, listened again, and then started pulling together so much helpful paperwork that I had to remind her that I didn't want to carry a library across her country. She culled the stack and then found me a small hotel a few blocks away, made the reservation, and wished me well. Despite plenty of packets, I left without any better idea of whether I could walk to the next town, whether the next town had any accommodations, or even whether farmers would welcome bedraggled wanderers. My questions were new to her and she had no answers.

Eighteen hours of travel do not leave my brain in the right condition to find a hotel that looks like every other house. A hotel in Scotland wasn't going to look like an American motel beside an interstate off-ramp. It wasn't going to be surrounded by an asphalt parking lot, or have a thirty-foot tall sign out front. I got lost. Someone steered me closer. I got lost again. Then someone steered me into the right winding street to Wilma and Jimmy's Ivy House, a white house that has more floors than I wanted to walk up and that has seen enough decades that I couldn't guess when it first was built. It was the end of tourist season, so they had lots of rooms available. They gave me the family room, the best room, the room on the top floor.

They must expect small families. The room was about half or one-third the size of most small motel rooms in the States. A motel along an interstate would provide a solo bicyclist twice as much room for about the same money. I didn't care. I was hungry and tired. I'd been wearing my hiking boots for 18 hours because it was the easiest way to pack them, despite the hassle back at the airport. I untied them, shrugged them off, and laid down for a nap. My feet were glad. A meal would wait. I almost fit on the bed. Welcome to Scotland.

When I woke up I looked out the window for the view but also to spot landmarks that would help me find the hotel again. Somehow I'd missed the supermarket across the road. I was tired enough to miss an acre of asphalt. The weather had cleared. The rain had stopped. I stumbled down the stairs that were built for smaller feet than my size 14s and went to find a restaurant.

Blog

I wanted fish and chips or shepherd's pie. I wanted Scottish food. But Scottish restaurants were closed in mid-afternoon, except for the bar part of the pubs and I wanted more than a beer for lunch. The Italian place was open. Welcome to Scotland. Have some Italian pasta, and some Irish Guinness.

Back up to the room for another nap, that woke me in time for dinner. My body clock was already tuning into local time.

I was still in a daze, but getting better. Jet lag and hours of travel can do that. The adjustment to a foreign country didn't look like it would be hard. I'd chosen Scotland for that reason. I was on a vacation, not a quest.

It was 2010, which meant it was possible to stay electronically connected, even across continents. There undoubtedly was an internet cafe around somewhere so I can email home and tell everyone where I was and how the trip had gone. I wasn't trying to brag. Most of my friends have had grander adventures. I knew that if I didn't keep friends and family informed that I'd be frequently reminded that I should. Facebook is handy. Besides, I'd also just signed up for eHarmony because I was tired of being single. My timing wasn't the best, but sometimes we work with the timing we're handed. I asked random people on the street about internet access and their directions eventually led me to the library five minutes before the staff had to give up the computers for an evening class. Paperwork must be filled out though, so a few minutes were spent authorizing me. With about two minutes on the clock, I blasted onto my accounts, dropped short messages into lots of waiting spaces, and then exited quickly throwing thanks over my shoulder as I made way for their students.

Time to try for an authentic Scottish meal again. Forget the fancy restaurants. Their choices were too expensive. I wanted pub grub, but the pubs only had beer. Finally I found a fish and chip shop before the evening rush. My belly wasn't totally on Scottish time yet, but food would help reset my clock. Imagery of fish dipped in batter being fried in oil sending aromas through the atmosphere was replaced with the person behind the counter reaching under the heat lamp to grab an already breaded and cooked fillet, set on a plate with chips, which was then delivered to my table with some attempt at service. The furnishings were one step up from mass-produced fast food joints. Hey, it's why I travel - to get real.

Dusk snuck onto the streets while I ate. The town was quiet, but that was either because I was a few streets over from a main road or because the ferry hadn't just disgorged a full hull of cars. Finding my way back was mostly luck, remembering where I was lost before, and aiming for an acre of asphalt. Losing my way usually helps me find it again later. Aiming at a big target, even if it was unappealing, helped me find the one I wanted to hit.

Back in the room I recuperated enough to finish unpacking and experience packer's remorse. Did I really need these boots? Why didn't I bring my favorite walking stick? I'd hit the stores in the morning for fluids that I couldn't carry on my flights. I'd also shop for a shovel handle as a cheap and sturdy walking stick. Eventually I'd figure out how to reliably turn on the hot water. My shower was cold. The bed was warm.

Start Walking

September 23
Stranraer - Ballantrae

Scottish singing started the morning, and it wasn't staged. The man of the house, which was correct because I as in a guesthouse and not a hotel, made and served breakfast with a song.

The house had been mostly empty. The few other guests were tied to the ferry schedule. They got in late and were gone early. Making eggs and bacon for one Yank wasn't going to be much of a chore. He'd done this before so he sang as he worked. I sat by a small window that framed an old church. The world felt mature, experienced, and settled.

I felt uprooted, naive, and surprised that I didn't feel atrociously jet-lagged. Breakfast was served at midnight Seattle time, and felt like it was right on time.

Sitting there I had no idea how far I'd get. The view of the countryside from my train ride wasn't encouraging. But the quick visit to the library ended with a few minutes with the man with the maps. There were trails along the coast; so, someone had at least planned for pedestrians along part of my route. The trails took the scenic route along the coast, but somewhere I'd have to turn inland. There were hints of trails but nothing definite. Well, that's the way I travel, aimed at a remote goal and willing to work out the details as they arrived. The first detail would resolve itself with the test of the first day. How far could I walk?

Fortunately, Scotland had a growing walking community and an interesting new twist to pedestrian law. As I understood it, a walker could walk almost anywhere, including across a farmer's field. That freedom was balanced with responsibilities. I could cross a pasture, but I had to make sure I closed the gates and didn't disturb the livestock. That was reasonable. I had no desire to stampede a herd. The farmer, though, didn't have to keep dogs on leashes and didn't have to post signs about bulls and rams. Scottish law expected us both to act responsibly while also allowing for liberties. Scottish law treated us both as adults. What a welcome change. Of course, that alone wouldn't make the trip work. I needed lodging and food every day, but it did open avenues. Shortcuts could happen.

I paid my bill and left after hearing a bit of the local gossip. The neighboring church was old and maybe the renovations weren't prioritized the way people expected. It was the sort of news that was easy to ignore as a tourist while being the evening's heated debate in the pub.

The doubts about my path were alleviated by geography. The route for the first day followed the shore of a bay. I could see the other side from Stranraer. It was far enough away that I couldn't tell if the buildings were hotels or offices, but I knew there was civilization; and probably also a bus route. If I didn't find a place to stay I could probably hop a ride back to the guesthouse. Adventures are fine, but security's nice too.

The walk out of town took less than an hour. The first few blocks put me back at the ferry terminal. A few blocks more took me to the suburb, singular. A few blocks more left me at the edge of vacant lots and beside farmer's fields. I'd followed a sidewalk that was a bike path, and then a shoulder, and then the top of a sea wall. The tide was out. People walked their dogs in the space between the water and the wall. Random bits of trash littered the mud, but it was typical for a seaside town. Somehow grocery carts end up trying to surf. The idea of walking from pub to pub was obviously not going to happen.

My doubts about my vacation choice hadn't changed, but I had to remind myself why I was in Scotland in the fall. It certainly wasn't for the weather. The clouds looked like the skies of home: Seattle grey, a chance that it might rain, but a possibility of sunbreaks too. The land was green and rolling beside salt water bays. Why did I travel eight time zones to walk foreign yet familiar lands? I could've analyzed the question into a headache, but travel becomes a story when it involves commitment. I was here. I was walking. The argument was moot, or at least easily shuffled back into my trusty subconscious.

I've run marathons, though they were years ago, but running 26.2 miles in four hours wasn't like wearing a pack and hiking boots. Without aches and pains, and with some training and support, maybe I could walk 262 miles in ten days. What I didn't know was how far and fast a jet-lagged body with stress-induced reminders of mortality could go when it was walking unsupported and laden with supplies. My record was encouraging, but my recent history was humbling.

During my quick visit to the library I'd checked the maps and Google's satellite photos of the surrounding geography. I'd learned two things. One was that the train had taken a route that was far inland from where I planned to walk, so the discouraging preview was easier to dismiss. The other thing was that the road to Glasgow wasn't much more populated than the train's route, so maybe that preview couldn't be dismissed. There were large and long gaps, but there was also hope because there were dots for towns along the way. Unfortunately, the maps were organized for people driving by car, or for walkers heading cross country. Walkers along roads were not a big enough market. I missed AAA, the auto club which had produced detailed maps and guidebooks that were excellent resources during my ride across America. Maybe some country pubs were waiting in the gaps between the dots.

The trip around the bay was shorter than I expected. Cairnryan arrived as a confidence boost, and a source of caution. I walked those 6.5 miles in about 2.5 hours. It wasn't even lunchtime and I'd made it to the first possible lodging. Stranraer was a city. Cairnryan was a collection of vacation cottages with a small convenience store and a large future. A new ferry terminal was being built on their side of the bay. If nothing else, they'd get a lot of traffic. I stopped long enough to realize that it was too early to stop, and that stopping there would be best if I had a car for running back into town for dinner or groceries. There weren't enough services for a walker. Candy bars and sodas from the convenience store would make a lousy dinner and breakfast.

There was a lot of day left, but was there enough to get to the next town? I felt fine, but the route had been flat. My map of Scotland had dots along the way, but dots don't mean hotels. Sometimes they only mean intersections and mailing addresses. The next towns and lodgings were either ten miles farther, or 24 miles farther, or I would be hunting for a bus stop. I didn't want to run out of energy without a place to stay, especially on the first day. That would feel like a bad omen. I'm a hiker. I had enough in my pack for an emergency bivouac, but I'd rather end at a pub and a bed. That daily itinerary conundrum was familiar. I've dealt with it on hikes and on the bike. The local shop owner wasn't much help. Everything was either just up or down the road for him because everything was measured in car miles. A few minutes in either direction took him to everything he needed. He never considered being stranded.

Shoulder up the pack and head out to the sidewalk along the shore again - and the pavement turned into a ditch surrounded by yellow tape and orange cones. That's the sort of travel advisory that never shows up at the information kiosk. The sidewalk and the road were being upgraded for the eventual ferry terminal. Eventually, that would be very welcome; but for me, it was a moat. One of the workers saw me and pleasantly walked me through the work site. He didn't have any advice either, but he knew about the coastal trail. I was on it, and it was about to leave the road to head up over a hill on an old carriageway. He wished me luck. The new road that went around a headland didn't have a sidewalk or a shoulder. I'd have to climb a hill. A notorious hill. My optimistic self remembered climbing Mt. Rainier more than twenty years earlier. My pessimistic self remembered having to stop four times to catch my breath climbing a hundred foot rise in my neighborhood within the last year. It looked like I'd be tested on my first day. Would I cruise up and over the hill with views to entertain me, or would I trudge and wonder if my heart would pop out of my chest?

He was right and I was glad he gave me directions. The road, busy with traffic and tightly bordered with guardrails, swept around a ridge of the hill and out of sight. Across the street at an intersection that looked like a driveway there was a trail sign. It pointed up a steep, but paved, farm road that was too narrow for two cars, and probably a squeeze for farm equipment. It was scenic, but I had a bad feeling about it. The worrier awoke and a short while later the body and brain negotiations began.

Photos of the path were iconic. Stonewalls older than any house back home, tended hillside pastures bordered with wild roses, a flock of pheasants scurrying out of my way, a view out across the bay and to the open sea. The land was a perch that defined the words view property. Put a pub there and people'd stay just to sit and sip and watch for days; but, there wasn't one. The hill was steep enough that any parking lot would've involved massive excavations or parking each car by chaining it to bedrock.

I passed from seaside strolling to struggled walking to forced breaks. I broke a sweat. My lungs began to get a workout. I tried slowing down but that wasn't enough. I retreated to an old exercise. Take fifty steps, then take a break. Repeat. There was no need to check my pulse. My heart hammered. Pretend that the stop is to take in the sights. Reinforce that image by taking out the camera. Wonder about why I'd create such a facade. Who was I performing for? An inquisitive farmer? Some internal judge and auditor? I needed oxygen, fluids, and fuel. Part of me was more worried about appearances where it was obvious that I was from out of town and out of breath. I didn't want to set a stereotype of an out-of-shape American tourist, but I knew something deeper was momentarily revealed. The moment passed. The road steepened. Fifty steps at a time were too many. Take forty. Take only thirty. Feel ridiculous. The climb was only about a 500-foot elevation gain. The hill behind my neighborhood back home is almost that tall. Both start at sea level. It can't be altitude sickness. It felt like my body had a few decades of deterioration, but it might have just been the results of pent-up stress and an internally forced march under the duress of high expectations and significant jet lag. I was hurting and humbled. And yet, if I met someone I probably would've found a way to laugh about it. An escalator, an elevator, how about a rope tow people?

A roadside sign told the story of the route. It was notorious for decades and probably centuries. Until the two-lane road was blasted out along the shore, the path scared travelers in slippery weather, and required extra teams of horses to keep wagons and carriages under control. The teamsters driving those wagons probably risked their lives on bad nights. Reading the sign was another excuse for me to wait long enough for my heart to settle back to thumping instead of hammering. I pretended to read slowly and intently. How was I going to finish this trip if I couldn't walk up a small hill?

One consolation was that I'd rather have a heart attack in Scotland than back in America. Non-US health care didn't carry the same dread of imminent bankruptcy that I got every time I considered going to the doctor. Of course, the only witnesses to an attack were the livestock and the fowl. I doubted that they'd run for help.

The path narrowed and the climb eased. A farmhouse went by. It used what level land was available. My feet rolled the earth past me as the scenery changed from steep hill climb to sloped rural stroll. Life improved when I was able to count to fifty without panting. My breath return and my pace increased. My body felt better but my mind was resetting goals. If not Aberdeen how about Edinburgh or Glasgow?

As my mind recovered the road dwindled. The asphalt turned to gravel and grass. It looked like I'd climbed the hill to find a dead end.

The road turned right. It bent like it hit a property boundary and geometrically changed my direction. It became a driveway. Following the asphalt would lead me to a house. That didn't look right. If I ignored the turn and went straight I'd be on a farmer's grass and dirt road that was headed to a gate in a fence. But another set of ruts suggested another pasture route. The image of finding a choice in life is engrained from Robert Frost's, The Road Not

Taken. ~~Some road was not going to be taken, but neither one was paved, neither looked well traveled, and there weren't any signs to tell me which way to go. Sometimes the choices aren't the main road and the road less traveled. Sometimes the choice is between two shrugs.~~ They were both unknowns and not handing out hints. The one that went straight headed to a fence and a gate at the crest of the hill. At least fence posts provided possibilities for trail markers. The other one headed off across hundreds of yards of pasture before finding forest. Maybe there'd be a cairn and a turn. I didn't know. I headed straight to the fence.

I knew that I was allowed to hike across a pasture. The little research I'd done had uncovered that fact because someone was very proud to prominently post it in various sources. Even if neither route had a sign, I could follow a compass heading and possibly bushwhack back to the road.

There was no need for a compass yet, because I found a small sign on the top of the post. I doubt that I could've seen from the road even if I knew to look for it. Regardless, there as a sign and I celebrated that. There was also a convoluted way to allow people through that would keep sheep from easily getting out. The first glance confused my tired mind and body. A few breaths later I conquered a puzzle built for livestock. Beyond the gate and the fence, following the sightline suggested by the arrow on the marker, was a view of more hills, no pavement, big puddles, lots of pastures, and no sign of civilization except that the forest had been cleared. My hill climbing wasn't complete. The route dropped into a ravine and I suspected that it climbed the opposite and equally high ridge. My heart wasn't encouraged.

Times like those were for mental noogies. Back home I'd spent more time deciding what to pack and less time researching my route. Maybe some route research would've been handy. The boots definitely were. My hiking boots were mountaineering boots stiff enough for heavy loads and crampons. They looked out of place walking around town, but I was glad I hadn't decided to wear my light, short hiking shoes. The rains that came down while I was on the train soaked the ground and drained away through rushing streams, but there was too much. The ground was saturated. Puddles were deep and long. The path was rutted. Farm equipment probably bounced whenever it went through. The day may have started neat and tidy, but within a hundred yards my boots had a new layer and mud splatters painted my pants to my knees. Shorter shoes would've been filled with mud. My gear was good. I doubted my wisdom. The sheep watched me walk by.

Cairnryan was only a couple of miles behind me. I guessed that it was almost ten miles to the next dot on the map. I felt like I was walking off into wilderness. It was the beginning of the second half of a longer than expected day. The next dot on the map, where the path intersected the main road, was Glenapp Church. The church was described as a tourist stop. I hoped I could stop there overnight. Hope is not exactly a strategy, but I worked with what I had.

Mud. Puddle. Uneven tufted tall grass. The sheep weren't doing their job. At least the puddles were an opportunity to rinse off my boots, and the grass acted as a brush.

It was easier walking in the pasture than down the tractor track. At the bottom of a drainage were a few stones barely rising above the surface of a swollen stream. Don't fall. At the least, falling would be embarrassing, probably messy, and with little hope of finding an evening laundry. At the worst, falling would be dangerous considering that a broken bone could strand me in a place that may not be visited for days. Ah, my vacation.

Such fears were common for me. My life had included a string of disappointments and postponed expectations. Compared to an Afghan tending a flock while bullets buzzed by, my life was luxurious. It didn't feel that way. At home I felt lonely. My portfolio was struggling amidst economic turmoil. Intellectually I knew that everything was temporary and that love and money would return, but my investment stresses and meager business success weren't easy to bear. My support network was the best in decades, but they had their problems too. My lifestyle was different enough that explaining my situation required substantial background briefings before a listener could get to the "Ah ha", or "I'm sorry to hear that" moment. Instead of understanding and compassion, I usually received boilerplate advice or admonition. Having no one to turn to during a nightmare night sometimes left me waking in fear. Fear became so common that I didn't recognize that it pervaded my days. The effects of the unrelenting stress eventually left me curled up on the couch for days at a time.

Enough of that. That was why I was on a vacation. I was putting myself into a rut because I knew the rut I had been in hadn't been healthy. Something had to change, so I changed my location and set a direction. I was in Scotland and walking across the country. If I worried every step I'd move too slowly and see the world around me.

Where was the next trail sign?

A stone wall led up and away from the stream. As it climbed the hill it bordered a forest instead of dividing a pasture. My guess was that the trail stayed in the clear. Sure enough, there was a trail sign at a gate. The arrow pointed into the empty pasture and away from any wall, fence, or landmark. A confusion of sheep trails scattered across the hillside. The arrow resolutely pointed towards a featureless, rounded and sloped ridge. Trusting the trail makers was a necessary step in making progress.

There was little else to give me confidence as I walked. My eyes scanned for trail signs or boot prints. No one else had walked there recently. Finally, just as I was about to lose sight of the sign I'd left, I saw hints of where to go next. Turn 45 degrees back towards the far fence and the forest. The detour through the field skipped the thick brush along the stone wall. Was it simply easier to plunk a post down in the middle of the pasture than it was to clear the brush and keep a straight trail? I'd hoped for a quick return to the next farm's road down to the highway. Instead I'd merely passed from sheep pasture to cattle pasture and another rise.

Somewhere along there was an apologetic or editorial paragraph stapled to a post describing a possible lack of quality control between one bit of the path and the next. It was probably at a property border. I got the impression that some ranchers weren't happy about the trail and had done the minimum required. The minimum was still better than having to cross the barbed wire and electric fencing that I'd expect in the States. The odd bit of trail may have been an expedient way to accommodate the trail, but it was more valuable as an insight into the local politics. Just because they passed a law and people followed it didn't mean they were happy about it.

The afternoon was aging. I was tiring. Occasional farm shacks and sheds were revealed as I passed around swells in the ground or the slight ridges. I considered using them as emergency bivouacs. The rats probably had squatter's rights.

Just when the ludicrous was beginning to sound reasonable and probable, my options improved. The buildings got bigger. Pavement reappeared. The next time the sign pointed into the fields and over a hill I ignored it. Asphalt was much more appealing. Instead of going where they said I should go, I thankfully walked down towards possible bus routes and civilization. At least I wouldn't be lost.

Blocking the one lane farm drive were a dump truck and an earth mover that were pointed downhill. The trucks were as wide as the road and I was staring at their back ends. The rain had damaged the ditch and they were repairing it with loads of gravel. There was no reason for them to look behind them. There was no way for me to get their attention. Swinging backhoe arms can hurt, and would probably launch me through the bush and down the steep slope to the road. I wasn't in that much of a hurry. Methodically they worked. Slowly I approached, singing and waving my arms. The dump truck driver didn't see me until I was nearly at his bumper. The back-hoe operator was too busy to notice and his rig was louder than my singing. It was a good thing that they had radios. The one called the other and they took a break for a few seconds. I surprised them. Evidently, walkers weren't common despite the news of the trail legislation and construction. I squeezed by without an explanation, only a wave. They went back to work.

A few hundred yards later I found the road again. It turned away from the shore to head inland and up a valley. At the intersection sat the traffic control member of their crew. He was the youngest and the most bored. Despite that, he barely moved and had little to say. His directions for lodgings were measured in how long the drive was to various pubs. Everything was less than a few minutes away, at highway speeds. That was no help. He didn't even know about bus schedules. At a guess the next place to stay was still either eight, ten, or 24 miles farther.

As I walked away, within sight of where he sat, there was an ancient stone mile marker with a 7 carved into it. I was seven miles from somewhere.

It was obvious why they steered walkers away from the road and onto trails through pastures. Even as the terrain allowed the road to gain elbowroom, the pavement didn't broaden to include a shoulder, a sidewalk, or even another lane. Guardrail hopping was my new dance step. I practiced walking on the right side of the road facing traffic and getting familiar with the cars driving on the left. Scoot around puddles. Step through tussocked grass. Try to not rip my pants on the sharp edges of metal rails. Wish for better brush maintenance. Overhanging bushes put me into strange postures and poses as I looked for traffic on the other side.

The road was officially a highway, or at least it was numbered. Full-sized tractor-trailers rolled by at top speed, which made it sound and look like a highway. But the two lanes were more like a West Virginia country road, curvy, determined, and constrained by geography. Walking was pleasant, as long as I concentrated on the view to my right and had no traffic on my left.

Miles passed, and eventually I found signs and then the building itself: Glenapp Church. Yes, it was a tourist destination, but for reasons that were only apparent by reading a travel brochure that I didn't have. Solid stonework, an old cemetery, a prime location situated above the road on drier land, no wonder it survived and was visited. Even without reader boards it had plenty of history to be read from the architecture. It didn't have any lodging though. Hopes and expectations postponed again.

The day was wearing and so was I. The weather was settling down to overcast and preparing for rain. The church was across from a trailhead and another road. I hadn't reached a destination, but I had reached a crossroad.

I was in the Ayrshire, a district with a coastal trail that had led me along a seawall then over hilly sheep pastures. I found another spur, or maybe I'd been lost before and had followed the wrong trail. In any case, I was at a trailhead that promised to take the scenic route towards Ayr. It made that promise and included a warning that high tides can close the trail. The sign advised me to consult my tide tables before proceeding. People familiar with coastal walks, especially in Washington State, know to take such warnings seriously. The Coast Guard regularly plucks scrambling hikers from deteriorating cliff faces that are rising from beachless shores that are assaulted by breaking waves and bone-crushing logs. The moon was almost full. The high tides would be high. I didn't have any tide tables. I wasn't going that way. The spur road didn't show on the map either. For all I knew it went a hundred yards and ended at a driveway. I was too tired to explore. The highway behind me was my only real choice.

So much for relying on civilization. There weren't pubs every mile or so. Those long stretches of rural I'd seen from the train were less civilized than what I walked through, but it still felt like walking a lonely road in Montana. Knocking on farmhouse doors wasn't likely because most houses were at the end of a long drives that left the highway and plunged out of sight, either over a ridge or around a wood.

Shoulder dancing continued, and tired legs had me worrying about weak knees twisting with the uneven ground. The day fell into a dull routine, my new rut, but an optimist knows that any situation can improve rapidly. An out-of-the-way traveler's house, or maybe a spot too new and small to have made it onto the map, could be around any corner.

The next town was Ballantrae, but there was a sign for someplace closer called Smyrton. Maybe, could there be, a place to stay without walking the extra miles to a dot on the map?

Fog turned to mist turned to rain. As I rounded a corner and found a sign for Smyrton I was already wet from waiting too long to put on my raingear. Optimism convinced me the rain was temporary, until it was too late.

Smyrton didn't look big. It wasn't. A collection of a few houses warranted a sign. The only homeowner outside grudgingly took some time from her busy schedule to tell me that there was no lodging in Smyrton. I had miles to walk. I thanked her for the dismal news. She thankfully got in her car to chase down her errands.

Around the next bend I caught glimpses of the sea and then a view of Ballantrae. The road swept back inland to contour around a valley sloping to the shore. My route was along a big bend with a broad view of the town of low buildings, the green valley, and the green waves. Stranraer looked like any harbor city. Ballantrae looked like the kind of town I was visiting Scotland to see. Despite the fine view, the possibility of getting dry, then clean, then fed, then rested hung in front of me. None of it would get closer unless I kept walking.

By the time I crossed the bridge that led into town, the rain had abated. It had been temporary and local. Ballantrae was dry.

Out of senseless resoluteness, I didn't pick the first B&B. I picked the second. I'd walked 17 miles with no lunch except three cheese sticks and one granola bar.

Seventeen miles. Only more than 200 to go, or maybe zero if I gave up. Ask a marathoner about running the next marathon just after having finished one. You may find that marathon is temporarily a dirty word. I was tired and I hadn't even finished a marathon's distance. In running shoes, with support, I'd run 26.2 miles in four hours. It took seven hours to walk 17 miles. It made sense that mud, boots, a pack, hills, pastures and jet lag each slowed me down, but it was humbling to realize how much.

After a nap, which was not negotiable, and a cold shower, where the shower was obviously necessary and the cold was a consequence of not knowing how to get hot water, I walked down the skinny main street of town. Main street was still the highway and still carrying highway traffic despite squeezing between houses and short businesses. The painted stucco walls looked like they were covering very old stone cores. The views were quaint and picture postcard. The audio was rural seaside quiet interrupted by rumbling diesels with loads that rattled across the uneven pavement. The sidewalks were narrow enough that I was amazed that trucks leaning into the turns hadn't shaved the eaves off the houses.

The owner of the B&B gave me directions to the library and the pub. Excellent. Except that the library was closing in 15 minutes, so the computers were turned off, and there wasn't an internet cafe despite the general comments made by the guidebooks. The pub was open, but wouldn't serve food for another hour. Ah, but at least I could have a Guinness. Ballantrae's schedule was out of synch with mine. I couldn't read. I couldn't eat. But I could drink. That's one way to test a culture's priorities. Back home I'd be able to get coffee anytime, though I didn't drink it, so the option doesn't do me much good. I didn't expect that my favorite Irish beer was so popular in Scotland, but I didn't complain. No other beer seemed interested in competing, and I wasn't driving anywhere. Bring it on. Did I want it normal? Normal wasn't ice cold. I surprised them by saying yes to normal. I like warm beer. Asking for a brain freeze never makes sense except on summer days in the desert, and even then it would be more than odd.

Walking into the pub startled me. Instead of an empty room and a quiet corner, about a dozen men and women were standing in a semi-circle centered on the door, beers in hand, with one space open as if the next person through the door would complete their circle. My first step in was followed by a stumble as every eye turned my way. They were surprised to see a tourist. I was surprised to be surrounded by a dozen people wearing black suits and dresses. It was either their version of office casual, or

I'd walked into a wake. Someone joked about the way I danced into the space. My tongue tripped out something about how I'd love to waltz but the music was the wrong beat, and I nervously stepped through their circle into the next room. Any gregarious aspect of my nature vanished. I felt like a naive American tourist and didn't want to reinforce the image. All I wanted was to find a seat and hide in the corner. Evidently my energy was so low that my social skills were gone.

One friend back home predicted I'd do that. She told me to be bold and sit at the bar and jump into the crowd. She's irrepressible. I was exhausted. I wanted to sit, quietly relax, enjoy my beer, and wait for the kitchen to open. My favorite and trusty dinner companions were along, a book and my notepad. Let me read and write and I will entertain myself for hours. Besides, I wanted to get a feel for pubs before making assumptions about what was appropriate and enjoyable.

The pub didn't fit any movie image, which wasn't a surprise. It was brighter than an American bar, but maybe that was because the sun was up and the windows pointed south and west. The drinking half was square with a square blocked out for the bar and the bottles. It had booths and stools that had more wood than upholstery. The eating half, where I sat in my corner by the kitchen door, was more open and spacious enough to include a snooker table that was the fun focus for four flirting younger folk. The three groups didn't meld or clash: the bar dozen, the hormone-driven gigglers, and me with my paper companions.

At last and at least dinner arrived and was Scottish: steak and Guinness pie. I was one of the first to order and one of the first to be served, but everyone's meals came out at about the same time. Within seconds after everyone was served the room went quiet as everyone ate in unison. I eat slowly, so the chatter began again before I was finished. The energy returned.

Sitting there watching the groups of friends clustered around tables I wondered about being alone. I didn't jump into their circles because, despite friendly admonitions, I am comfortable being alone. I'd prefer to be with a partner. There were good reasons to walk with my friends Brian and Jonathan. There was also the romanticized notion of strolling across country with some wonderful woman. Good ideas, but logistics and luck didn't work out this time.

Besides, who else would want to walk across Scotland without following itineraries? I walk into the unknown on a regular basis, even when I'm not on vacation. Physically, financially, or philosophically, I have less fear than many about picking a direction and a general goal. I worry the details as they arrive. We don't know the rules of the world. We have guesses, but even our equations for gravity have room for improvement. Our statements about finances always include caveats. Pronouncements about philosophy can be stated with confidence and emphasis, but they are opinions, not facts. Unknowns are part of my world. Who else would be willing to step into these same unknowns?

The next few weeks would involve a lot of stepping, as long I could find a route. After dinner I realized that there was something more and less to walking than stepping. Walking is walking. Walking is a simple state of being that was also moving meditation. Most vacations show people sitting, but sitting still would give my mind too much time to wrap itself around into circles, twists, then knots. Lots of other vacation are more active, which I've enjoyed, but I had doubts that my body would survive it. Besides, frantic activity can be tiring, and is only relaxing for me if taken to a cathartic extreme like on my ski vacations. Walking is simple movement, steady, and repetitive. Breathing is repetitive. The repetition defined the new rut. My mind only had to be engaged enough to dodge traffic and find routes. Any remaining mental or physical energy can be layered on for fun. I wasn't there yet. My mind was working too hard worrying about logistics and my motivations. That extra effort would fade as I settled into my new routine. Would I enjoy anything more, or less?

I was tired, but I was doing better than I expected. The morning's fear was already slowly eroding. Maybe the Guinness helped.

Enjoys Long Walks On The Beach

September 24
Ballantrae - Girvan

Breakfast was a rerun: scrambled eggs, bacon that was more like weak ham, wheat products that my body didn't like, juice, tea, and a sincere chef and host; just like back in Stranraer. Before I left he showed me why my shower was cold. For safety and frugality the hot water is only turned on when it's needed. I wondered what that switch switched. The hot water had to be turned on for that bathroom and then the hot water faucet would do something useful. If I'd asked earlier I would have been more refreshed, but I didn't want to show too much ignorance after my questions about why the toilet was only working halfway. The American tourist couldn't conquer plumbing.

The weather looked better. At least my rain gear would ride inside for a while. The signs said the route followed the coast. That sounded scenic. I trusted the road more; but I couldn't give up the trail so readily - especially when it promised to start as an early morning beach walk. The signs led down to a broad, sometimes pebbly, sometimes sandy, beach. Luckily the tide was out. There was enough elbow room to park jets. The free space on either side was a relief after the highway. The level beach was a treat after a muddy pasture. A wind cleared the sky, but the gusts picked up sand that stung and tried to scour my face. I put on sunglasses even though I didn't have to squint.

For more than a mile, over a hundred feet of shore was exposed between breakers and grass. A few folks walked their dogs. The majority of the scenery was familiar. My photo essays of Whidbey Island are made from walking similar beaches watching for plays of light, or arrangements of rocks and shells. Ballantrae's beach was much less sheltered. It looked across the wild and open Irish Sea. The sea was rough enough for breakers, but probably not enough for surfing, and undoubtedly smooth compared to a storm. The sand was soft and took more effort to walk across, but it didn't suck at my boots or try to twist an ankle. The pebbly patches were firmer, but would sometimes shift as if the pebbles were pile of bad ball bearings. Any rhythm was interrupted within a few dozen yards. Dune grasses created tiny tufted islands that anchored mini-ridges of sand that collected random bits washed in with the tide. Everything was low, below knee height, evidence that the waves regularly cleaned the beach. The main difference with my beaches back home was the lack of driftwood. Occasional chunks were randomly placed, but the hills and shores had fewer forests and trees to contribute a fresh supply.

Unnatural bits were there too. It was easy to ignore the plastic. There was less than I expected considering oceanic garbage patches. The front-end loader was harder to ignore. A local needed sand and gravel. He drove his earthmover down to a convenient bit of beach, pointed the back end to the sea, and shoveled up a cubic yard or so of good concrete supplies. Back in the USA that would be a police blotter moment for trespass and maybe environmental assault. In Scotland it looked pragmatic and only slightly out of place. None of the dog walkers seemed to mind.

Ballantrae became an abstraction on the horizon. A mile or two of beach later, as I was falling into the cliché of "enjoys long walks on the beach", the end of the sand came into sight. A stone house lived between the end of the beach, above the high tide line, at the base of another hill, and to the side of the highway. It looked practiced at weathering storms. Maybe it was the shepherd's house for the pasture that climbed above the cliff. The beach vanished into a rocky headland. An extension of the trail passed along the shadowed base of a craggy cliff. A sunnier route headed to the top of the hill, where it probably had phenomenal views; but the climb looked to be steeper than the one by Cairnryan and that had been bad enough. The highway met the trail at the house, and then climbed to a shorter pass inland. I was walking Scotland to relax and commemorate my bicycle trip, not to impress anyone, not to win an award, and not to prove anything to anyone. I watched myself consider the natural and scenic routes. The cliff and the pasture routes were worthy of story and picturesque, but I just wanted to take it easy and not get lost or over-exerted while trying to get to the next beer and bed. I wasn't there to write a book or produce an exhibit. Ignoring all of the self-imposed societal pressures, I realized that what I wanted was a nice walk.

Taking the highway felt like a cheat, but I was going to cheat. That small defiant moment made me aware of something I couldn't identify. What or who was being defied? Some people would step back, find a spot on the beach to meditate and maybe journal about the moment. I recognized the excellent opportunity for self-analysis and personal growth. My back brain got busy. The rest of my brain left it to its internal machinations. Psychoanalysis could come later. I was on vacation. I walked.

Modern highways are much saner climbs than ancient carriage ways. Horses would appreciate the difference. Cars with hundreds of horsepower are oblivious. I'm human. I have less power than a horse. I stopped for a few breaks which were much more casual than the day before, and were also excuses to take pictures. Highways, interstates, and rail lines, are mechanistic, dirty, and distracting. Many people see them are ugly slashes across the world. I simply look at the untouched part of the world. There was beauty regardless of the path we've paved through nature.

Pastured meadows layered themselves ridge folding behind ridge to a fading green horizon. Ancient stone walls and modern wood fencing squared off sections and acted as anchors for bushes and small trees. A forest may have been cleared to make the pasture, but pastoral was still pleasant. It would remain low and green as long as the livestock trimmed the grass and somehow discouraged any seedlings. The few trees grew stunted, cowering in the persistent wind. I couldn't blame them. If I was stuck out there in the field, I'd be hunkered down beside the stoutest stone wall I could find.

Standing at the crest of the hill was a relief. My heart recovered nicely. Maybe jet lag explained a lot. A bit of my confidence returned.

Those days of rain were a blessing . The view up and back along the coast was cleared. The horizons were pushed back and I could see where I'd woken and where I was headed and hoping to sleep. I'd already lost sight of Stranraer where I'd started. Progress was easily made as long as it was steady. Ahead I saw a town that didn't look nine miles away. Maybe I'd manifested an early lunch. I could tell that someone had manifested a gorgeous day, and the path before me was headed downhill along a green shore. Views like those are worth millions.

Even 11AM was too early for lunch. Walking into Lindelfoot before noon was an accomplishment and an encouragement. The town was quaint, which is another way of saying it was small. A few buildings weren't enough to entice me to stop on such a gorgeous day.

Another stone mile marker was chiseled with Girvan 9. I guessed that Girvan was 9 miles away, at least by the old road, wherever that was. Nine kilometers would be a better answer, but I doubted that it was a kilometer stone. Logically the distance was reasonable, but emotionally I wanted someplace closer. For my second day of walking I wanted to reach town at lunch, have fish & chips & Guinness, then check into a room for a nap, a dinner, and an easy evening. That wouldn't get me across Scotland quickly though. I said I was going to cross the country on pedestrian power, and I didn't want to fail. Besides, I'd feel guilty about stopping so early. I arrived in Lindelfoot early. Maybe Girvan would be easier to get to than I thought too.

Girvan is big enough that I saw it miles before I got there. With a better trail, or even just a wider shoulder, it would've been easy to spend more time enjoying the view. Long views of green grass abutting blue water were sweet. Add in nice weather and extend the trail around the entire island and there'd be plenty of pedestrian traffic. Unfortunately, the shoulder was narrow and the traffic was busy, so I spent more time watching for cars than appreciating vistas. The real trail was probably nicer, but not as likely to get me to beer and a bed with time to spare.

Back in Ballantrae, someone gave me advice about where to find a hotel in Girvan. He suggested following the highway as it curved into town. That didn't sound scenic, but it did sound convenient for things like libraries and bookstores. At the edge of town the highway curved away from the water, just as he said. At least he gave good directions. But, I also found a trail marker. I'd stumbled onto the coastal trail again even though I never saw an intersection. The road and the trail converged as the asphalt got closer to the waves. The sign contradicted my directions by pointing to the waterfront. Being from a waterfront town, I knew that hotels would line up along the water to give the tourists the best views, unless the expensive homes beat them to it. That sounded appealing. Besides, I didn't want to walk into town and then lose the trail. The trail existed for walkers. I might as well see if it worked for me.

The trail followed the shore. That wasn't a surprise. As the highway peeled away my walk became easier and quieter. Sidewalks and pedestrians showed up. Life looked good. I saw a chance for a late lunch at a diner on wheels, fish and chips to go. A few hundred feet before I got there a tour bus stopped. Its brakes hissed, the bus settled, and the doors opened to disgorge dozens that formed a line long enough to encourage me to keep walking. I'd probably be able to get to lunch in a pub by the time they all got served.

The shore and sidewalk turned into a broad expanse with enough room for walkers, bicyclists, strollers, and pets. To the left was a seawall that didn't block the view of the sea or the tide-exposed beach. To the right was a wide walkway that bordered an immaculate, lightly rolling lawn populated by kids, ambling elders, and frisbee-chasing dogs. Farther back were row houses with no gaps between the buildings, and no sign of a hotel; except one, which had a No Vacancy sign that steered me away. Except for the sign, it was a welcoming setting, but my world view was mildly shaken. Evidently tourism didn't command a view and maybe the only hotels were back along the highway. My legs grumbled up at my brain. What now thought box?

Ever the optimist, I convinced myself that there'd be other hotels farther along the rest of the waterfront. Girvan is a city, a city with a great view, there must be lots of choices. Girvan also has a small harbor and a sign for the tourism information center. I walked around the one to get to the other, only to find that the info center had turned into a shop. Ah, but the golf course is on the far end of town. Certainly it would have rooms. I might have to change clothes to meet some dress code just to register, but it could be worth the effort. Nope. No need to worry about the dress code. The course and its site were worthy of a resort, but the golfers assured me I'd have to walk back into town. There were no rooms at the inn, and no other inns along the water.

Thanks for slow mechanics. As I dragged myself back to the harbor I met a woman who was walking laps around the blocks, killing time waiting for her car to be fixed. We walked. We talked. She wasn't from around there and didn't know where to stay either. She knew where the tourist info was though and was happy for to have a goal. She led me right back to the same re-purposed shop that I'd found. At least she tried, and her company distracted my mind from my tired legs.

On the other side of the harbor I walked alone, hoping for serendipity to reveal a hotel, B&B or pub with rooms. I wound up back at the only hotel I'd seen. I was drained, and considering finding a taxi or a bus. I knocked on the hotel door and waited. The sign said "No Vacancy" but maybe they'd know where I could get a room. A short while later the owner answered my knock. She admitted that her discouraging sign was one way she had of relaxing a bit after she'd booked enough guests to cover the expenses. Of course I could come in and stay. What did I want for dinner? I could stop for the day. The room was welcome. I'd found hot water, but not a shower. Instead there was a tub that was almost big enough, but not really. I could get clean, but I'd have to find some other way to relax. That was alright. A good meal and a drink would help a lot.

I dined alone. The restaurant was empty. She gave me the bay window seat which would have been romantic for a couple. The view was enough to entertain. It was the park. The lawns were kept immaculate for putting practice. The swing sets were modern and colorful. The decorative pool was clean and artfully built into curves wrapped with sidewalks and benches. The sea view was out of view behind slight waves that had been built into the land to keep the park from being flat and dull. One island was tall enough to be visible. It housed a quarry for curling stones. It looked a bit like one, and the shape nearly matched the structural curve of the very modern swing set. Symmetry was at work.

While I watched the view, my thoughts roamed: why was I here alone, how all the good looking women were back home, when would I turn inland and east, how did people pass the time before books or television became popular? The park was busy, but an entire city sat behind me. Was almost everyone simply sitting in front of their televisions? I wanted a book, but I hadn't stumbled by one and I wasn't going on a grand adventure after so many miles.

The moon was almost full. I sat there, picking my way through a meal that had three versions of potatoes then a dessert of a second beer. It was only my second day of walking but I felt myself falling into a new, soon to be familiar, pattern; a new rut. If it had all been planned, I'd be worrying too much about reservations and itineraries. Maybe that's why the transition was so easy. I wasn't forcing myself into a rigid pattern. Instead I was relaxing into a habit. I was relaxing.

Out across the lawn, kids ran, teenagers strolled slowly enough to keep from sweating and upsetting their style. Pets were being collected and herding dogs were quickly commanded back into cars as the sun set.

A culture defines itself by what it maintains meticulously and what it ignores. The grass, the regulations, the playground, the seawall, the working dogs, the BBC were all tight. The cigarette butts, the loud music, the lack of greens in a diet, the slow decay in many of the buildings, the lax logic in some political and stereotypical attitudes were loose enough that I felt more comfortable keeping quiet and enjoying my beer.

What was I meticulous about? What was I loose about? Was there any of that I wanted to change? Were there changes that were necessary, or was I trying to aim at too restrictive of an abstract standard?

After the sun set, I went up to my room, enjoyed some BBC, missed having a good book to read, and marveled at an ad for a sandwich made from two pieces of bread and lots of bacon. Bacon sandwiches are a childhood comfort food that never entered my adult diet. My favorite sandwich in college was a BLT without the LT. There was something repulsive and appealing about the ad. I was glad to see some traditions continue and had no desire to participate. I decided to decide about my route when I got to Turnberry, six miles up the road. As the television swung into something I didn't want to watch, I picked up my pen and began to write until it was time to sleep.

Danger Do Not Enter

September 25
Girvan - Maybole

What happened to jet lag? I woke just after sunrise as if I'd spent weeks acclimating. Even without jet lag shuffling my schedule I should've slept in after that much walking and so little sleep. I spent the night on the edge of leg cramps, frequently waking up to quickly massage away a twitch. Usually they show up from a muscular chemical imbalance, but something had kicked in a midnight anxiety attack. Maybe my brain tried conjuring a sprain. I didn't sleep well, but I up in time for breakfast.

Breakfast. Some things never change. Scrambled eggs, hammy bacon, toast I couldn't eat, tea I couldn't drink, and some juice. Pack up. Pay up. Thank my hosts. Start walking.

Stereotypes get reinforcement because they tend to include a bit of truth. My Scottish morning started with a walk around a harbor populated with early sailors, and along a golf course attracting early risers. The people most likely to be out and active were either working or playing. The only things missing were fog and bagpipes.

The sea was close but I couldn't see it. The trail signs led me to the land side of a sand dune; so, instead of watching water I walked on a golf cart track which followed a fairway. The view wasn't as nice, but it wasn't bad either. Besides, a signed and paved track was much more appealing than hilly and muddy sheep pastures.

Town was left behind within minutes. The golf course didn't take much longer and soon the trail entered farmland. The trail merged with a farm road, which was gave me lots of room and no traffic. It was a fine route until it took a sharp turn into a farmyard surrounded by walls, sheds, and garages. Maybe I was allowed to cross pastures and fields, but I was hesitant to walk into a business' work area out of respect for their privacy and desire to stay out of their way. Walking across a remote pasture isn't as intrusive as getting between the forklift and the hay bales. At least I knew I wasn't lost. A sign asked walkers to be quiet, so they expected and accepted walkers.

Old farmyards may have been muddy and filled with chickens and goats. This farmyard was more like walking through an organic factory, everything organized with lots of parked machines.

The aroma hadn't changed. Livestock were about, but maybe they were effectively parked and garaged too.

The trail took me back towards the water and I relaxed. I didn't want to get in the way of farm tractors and health inspectors. I also wasn't worried about being lost. The highway and the shore would bound my route for miles until Turnberry. At Turnberry the road split into a coast road that promised scenery and maybe history, and an inland road that pointed at my backup plan, a train station. My mind has less to do for a few hours because I didn't have to make any decisions until I got to the intersection.

Some stereotypes failed. I'd been told that there were plenty of places to stay in Scotland. The next one was never far away, so I'd heard. I think those folks were in cars or taking trains. I hadn't found a hotel guide that was organized well enough for the total stranger like me. One brochure had a string of place names, which is great if you know the area or if there's a map dotted with locales. I had a map with dots for cities and a book with hotels but the two weren't made for each other. Specific addresses would never show on a map large enough to encompass my route. I'd made it across America by carrying auto club maps and guidebooks that tied together nicely. Thank you Automobile Association of America. Was there a WAS, a Walkers Association of Scotland? The well known and frequently used trails probably had everything I'd need; but I was following my own path, finding my own way, walking into an unknown that I'd chosen.

Trail markers were my best bet for detailed directions, but there weren't enough of them. Well-signed trails have markers at every intersection. The best trails have signs past the wrong turns so travelers know they made a mistake. Such trails are rare, so I wasn't surprised to find intersections that were sign-less. The trail makers probably thought the markers were obvious. Maybe the trail had all of the necessary signs for everyone else, but not for me. I managed to get lost.

The rough farm pavement went to the right and towards the highway, but was headed inland. To the left was a farm road that was pointed in the right direction, but it was mud and puddles. I stopped. I snacked. I sipped. I realized that there was no way to find out which was correct except to try one. Pavement sounded like a better, or at least cleaner, idea. I walked towards the highway for a bit, thought I saw an underpass and remembered farm roads crossing under highways to get to inland uphill fields. After a hundred yards I turned around and walked onto the puddled path.

Meandering loses its appeal when it is merely more time spent in doubt. The route swept wide, sometimes within sight of the sea, sometimes bending around a field. After what felt like half a mile I passed a short equipment tower and found a farm gate blocking the path. On the other side was deep green pasture. Cattle may have used the land but there was no sign that anyone on two legs had walked there. Maybe the ground was so fertile that the grass grew faster than walkers could trample it into a path. If it was the trail there should be a trail marker. I saw the back of a sign attached to a gate. I leaned over the gate, hoping to read the upside down version of "Trail This Way". Instead it was, "Danger. Do Not Enter." Oh great. So the last half mile had been through Danger. The cattle in the field had a sign saying Do

Not Enter. Back at the intersection with the road there was nothing. My guess was that the trail was back there and that I didn't want to stand where I was. Maybe that equipment tower beside the gate was less benign than it appeared.

Following the puddles back to the intersection and out to the road was tedious because backtracking is a waste of time and an admission of a mistake. Besides, I was watching for danger as I walked back to the road.

Eventually, I found more trail markers. The pavement aimed at the highway, but the trail turned to parallel the traffic. At least I wasn't lost. The cars drove on smooth asphalt. My route was through the neighboring pastures, staying to the uneven, grassy side of the barbed wires and stone walls.

From a distance stone walls look solid, but stone walls weaken. They're built from the stones in the land, which is convenient and a handy way to get them out of the field. Stones aren't very perishable, but without something to hold them together, piles of stones eventually tumble. They were used for centuries, but they require sweaty maintenance. The farmers had given up. Beside most stone walls were more modern fences. Barbed wire is strung quicker than stones are stacked, but wire rusts and eventually must be repaired too. It only has to be bought every time it is installed or replaced, but money must be made and spent. An electric wire inside the other two was newer, more expensive, and required power; but it was easier to put up. All three walls stood in parallel. Subsequent ages and technologies stepped from self-reliance to being connected to a common economic and energy grid. I don't know which was the most effective, but I do know that the remnants of the rocks will outlast the newer two.

Eventually I got tired of picking my way through bumpy pastures. The shoulder beside the road was paved, and when it disappeared the ground beside the road was no less rutted and ankle twisting than the pasture.

A light-industry building and a tourist stop were some of the few breaks in the rural character. Scotland, like any country, doesn't have to fit into neat niches of purely urban and purely rural; except for maybe places like Monaco.

Turnberry arrived with speed warning stripes, three stripes for slow, two stripes for slower, one stripe for slowest. I didn't change my speed.

It wasn't even noon, and the weather looked like the tourism brochures had taken over. Miles should pass effortlessly under such skies. I'd found accommodations in town, but I didn't want to stop. The daily question was, if I go farther will I find a place to stay? There were two choices: head along the coast to Dunure and its touristy ruins, or inland towards the rail line at Maybole. Walking without an itinerary, picking a path without a plan, meant a lot more flexibility and also a lot more time spent making choices. I could go anywhere I wanted, but I had to make sure I got somewhere. My breaks were interrupted. I'd start by enjoying the views or diving into introspections, but my brain would wander into guessing about which way to go. Neither route was guaranteed. At least traveling solo meant my choice would only affect me. Fortunately, someone built a properly placed tourism information billboard. It had lots of enticing suggestions but very little useful information. I couldn't tell if the places called out were towns, ruins, or resorts. Rushing wouldn't help. Standing there didn't help either, but at least for a while my brain and body switched roles. My brain worked while my body rested.

I suppose a mistrust of the road less taken that ended me in a pasture steered me to the highway instead of the coast. Besides, I enjoy seeing the way people live more than the cleaned up version of how we think it was centuries ago. Inland and Maybole looked more real. Dunure and its ruins were history, interesting for sure, but an older story. A better chance of lodging helped me relax, and relaxing was the goal of the vacation.

Travel. See the world, and how else could I come across a sign for an otter crossing. Otters! The exclamation point made it look like a celebration instead of a warning.

Pass the otter exclamation, and head up the hill. The walking was easy along sidewalks and shoulders as I turned my back to the sea and the possible luxury of Turnberry Resort. The resort didn't register until I was a mile away. Supposedly it was a short bit up from the intersection on the coastal road. I suspected I wouldn't meet their dress code, but there was something else in my mind that didn't want me to go there. I accepted the intuitive nudge and kept walking.

It was a fine fall afternoon, a prime day for walking. Most of it was rural, but I walked through a town that was apparently devoted to a poet. Scotland seemed to be proud of its poets but was sparse when it came to bookstores. My reading material was sketchy. Someone left behind the same Dan Brown novel in a couple of places. Maybe a literary agent was taking a cue from the Gideons and their bibles.

My personal tour of the countryside was more than entertaining. Ancient abbeys, castles, and landmarks crept by. Some were cleaned up for tourists. Many were waiting for either repairs or collapse. It was obvious that trying to save everything would bankrupt the country. Immaculate preservation of history is impressive, but the effort can stymie progress. The past is valuable but so is the present and the future. Scotland has been lived in for centuries. Every lineal foot could claim a sign or a marker. Lives work that way too. I considered my past and my possible futures, and wondered if I wondered about them too much, too little, or just enough.

Reaching Maybole ended a long afternoon that left few other memories. My legs tired before town arrived. Town arrived, but without lodging. A pub appeared, but without rooms. I didn't care. I blundered in and found myself the center of another semi-circle of attention. The sudden stop and communal interest was abrupt enough that common manners were already scattered, so I just launched into asking for help. They only knew of one place in town that rented rooms, if they were even still open. There was a B&B on the far side of town. They wished me well and I stepped back onto the sidewalk.

Maybole looked like a movie set. Buildings abut buildings along the highway that funneled itself into the main street. The street, the sidewalk and the walls formed a rectilinear valley of concrete and stone. It felt narrow, and narrowed when two trucks passed in opposite directions. The space between the shops and the traffic felt confining, especially in contrast to the recent miles of countryside. I couldn't see the horizon. Archways led to practical courtyards.

Alleys and narrow side streets curved out of sight. With a grey sky and a misty fog it would be a great setting for a cold war spy movie.

The far end of town is always a bad set of directions. The only way to know the far end has been reached is to walk past it. Finally the buildings had air between them. Houses became more contemporary. Was the far end at the end of the old or the end of the new? I passed a few intersections. Was the end along a different road? I was running out of energy but not out of doubts. I kept to the main street and the density continued to decrease. Eventually houses made room for farm buildings and I wondered if I should turn back. It was good that I'd gone just that bit farther. Across the street from a pasture was a B&B sign. A nice couple were outside painting. It was the end of the season, so, yes, this was the time to fix up the place while the weather was still nice; but no, they weren't closed yet, and yes, I could have a room. Dinner, oh it was almost all take-away and back in town, about a half a mile. Good news about the bed and the room. Bad news about the walk.

I went into my room, dropped my pack, rested enough to retrace my steps looking for the Chinese takeout that she recommended. Instead I found the internet, which was only available Monday through Friday, and what I believe was Italian take away. No bookstore. No movie theater. No pub along my dinner walk. I settled into an evening of Dan Brown, the BBC, and listening to the trains running along the tracks at the back of their property. Evidently an escape route was closer than I expected because the B&B's neighbor was the train station.

Introverted Outside Extroverted Inside

September 26
Maybole - Prestwick

Decisions. Decisions. A choice had to be made. There was no obvious best way to get to Aberdeen. My route could go as far east as Edinburgh, which was appealing because I'd heard very good things about it, but then I'd have to cross a firth on a very long bridge headed north. The problem with some bridges is that they're only for cars, and I didn't want to walk into a "No Pedestrians" sign. I could go nearly north through Glasgow, but I'd already been there and some folks had warned me about certain neighborhoods that I probably wouldn't recognize until I was standing in them. My preferred compromise was to aim for the less urban areas between the cities. It was closer to a diagonal and would keep me away from "Don't Walk" signs. A bicycle path up the middle would be great. The next city along Maybole's highway was Ayr. All of my choices diverged from that crux. Luckily, there was a also tourism information icon beside Ayr's spot on the map. Decisions could be shelved until I got there. I was about 180 miles from Aberdeen. Bit by bit I'd get it done. All I had to do was walk.

Fall left a big hint in the morning. Heavy frost whitened the pastures to the horizon. The seasons progressed. Maybole dropped behind quickly. My chill didn't last long, but I also don't remember much of the morning. Maybe I was colder than I thought. At two and a half miles an hour I reached the city of Ayr far before lunch. Finally I found a place with plenty of street food, or at least fish and chips that I could eat while walking, but I was too early.

Ayr was paved streets, traffic, sidewalks, tall buildings, clean shops, and vacant graffitied storefronts - a typical city. The tourism information shop was most of the way into town. Its signs drew me along, which meant I swept past window shopping and browsing. If I'd found the "i" early I would have spent more time looking at the displays. My decision gate was my goal and until I reached it I didn't want to be distracted. I noticed the city life, felt separate from it, and had no desire to engage with it. My pace was slow, steady, and quietly determined.

City life swirled with freneticism as people rapidly chased through their lists of tasks or randomly bounced between shops. I wasn't relaxed either, but I was glad to have a much simpler list of goals. Which way should I go? Which way did I want to go? Which way would I enjoy? Could they all be the same?

The woman at the tourism information store was sincere and enthusiastic. She was warm and friendly and extroverted, but not very helpful. I asked questions she didn't hear often or at all. Which routes had lodging between the big dots on the map? Which routes were best for walking? Were there neighborhoods that a walker should avoid? She had advice for walkers, but it was hikers' advice for the established cross country routes in the south or the wilder areas in the north. She also had advice for city travelers, but it was based on cars and buses. I talked into a gap in her knowledge.

It wasn't even noon, so I wasn't going to sit still. Of the three routes I was considering, the only one that I knew had lodging within a few miles was the route that was aimed at Glasgow. It looked like I'd get to walk along the sea for one more afternoon as I headed to Prestwick. That sounded pleasant. My choices that seemed so varied and that were aimed at a target hundreds of miles away, were reduced by the simple near term need of finding a room for the night. Grand plans are wonderful brain exercises, but daily pragmatism can get the biggest vote. I hoped that a long list of pragmatic choices generally pointed at a far off goal would get me across the country.

As I left the city center I found a walk-away fish and chips lunch. For the first time I'd have three meals in one day! Fish and chips handed to me from under a heat lamp in exchange for a few pound coins.

Iconic and unremarkable cuisine took me through paved suburbia quickly. Eating distracted me as I walked. I barely noticed the food or the scenery. All of my energies went into trying to chew and navigate at the same time. The route from Ayr to Prestwick is paved with sidewalks, shops, signs, distractions, and opportunities to go the wrong way because there was finally more than one road. Choices, the curse of urban life. By the time I finished lunch and settled on a route I was almost done for the day.

Neighborhoods rolled by instead of farms. Stone walls bordered crushed rock, planters, and pets instead of pastures, shrubby trees and sheep. There were people on the sidewalks. I actually made eye contact in Scotland. That was rare, or at least not as common as back home on Whidbey. I'd been told that the Scots were introverted outside and extroverted inside. The pubs seemed that way, but it wasn't until Ayr that I noticed the outdoor reticence.

I made it to Prestwick before 1PM. With the extra time I aimed for the far end of town, which I now recalled from checking airline prices. There was an airport in Prestwick. I almost booked a flight into there instead of Glasgow. For all I knew, Prestwick was as big as Glasgow but not as well known. It was hard to tell from the pull-down menu on a reservation web site. The walk across town was long enough to be urban but short enough that I soon saw the airport. That was comforting. When in doubt, especially when hunting for internet access and travel information, I try to find a hotel by an airport. They tend to have the services a traveler requires at the expense of, expense and an unappealing view. But I'm an aerospace engineer. I like airports.

I also like views. There was a seaview hotel beside the open space that was a golf course. Good view, recreational facilities, close to the airport, of course, it was the priciest room of the trip so far; but it also looked like the most relaxing. I considered walking farther, but I'd already covered 12 miles and had the impression that the next lodging was about six miles farther, not just on the other side of the airport. It was time to relax. Repeat and remind: It was a vacation, not a chore. I was doing this because I wanted to, not just because my health told me I should, even though it had cast a strong vote.

At least this time view wasn't just from the restaurant, but from the room too. The hotel back in Girvan had a great view, but my room had looked at other buildings. Despite the price the room was Euro-small. There was enough room to air clothes as long as I didn't mind napping between them. The restaurant was waterfront dining with table linens and fancy menus. Dinner was a steak and a Guinness instead of steak-and-Guinness pie. It was refreshing to need a knife and fork. I felt a bit out of place around fancy napkins and a squadron of tableware. My table was in the corner by the window, which everyone avoided for some reason. The waitress seemed to appreciate being able to visit the less-hectic side of her space.

The view and the food were great and a bonus, but the real draw was their computer. They promised free computer use and internet access. I missed my friends and wanted to update my blog. Rather than hide the electronics in some conference room or in the middle of the lobby, they'd repurposed an old wooden phone booth. In place of a phone was a computer. It was a stylish, private, and quaint way to touch my electronic home. Unfortunately it had no appreciation for the ergonomics of seating a six foot blogger, and phone booths weren't designed to accommodate keyboards, mice, or wrist rests.

My walk across Scotland was not turning into a marathon pub crawl. The gaps were too long. But that was no reason to miss an opportunity to try again. I went back to the bar and ordered a whisky, my first of the trip. My return for my 75 ml dessert was a lot like a visit to any hotel bar. It wasn't a pub adventure. Almost everyone was elderly and sitting properly at table, or businessmen settling themselves into personal isolation. Some people continued to live within World War II and it was still dinner conversation. Their gender roles hadn't changed. She ordered a white wine; but he countermanded that because he knew that she really wanted sherry. They brought her sherry. A screenwriter sat at the bar to avoid sitting amidst dialogue that he'd be too keen to capture. It would pop him back into work mode, and he said so loudly enough that I and others heard it. Late diners making chaotic requests made the waitress turn towards me, roll her eyes, and softly mouth the words, "Only six months until retirement."

My brain relaxed. The condition of my house, my car, my portfolio, and my computer were moot. Writing turned from a compulsion, a should, and a defense against loneliness into an easy entertainment, something I wanted to do. Other things relaxed: my attitude, my pace, my expectations. Maybe the whisky helped.

If I wasn't reading or writing I was looking at the map. My route was a puzzle that had one less piece at the end of each day. With a new day's knowledge and my self-imposed goal, where would I go tomorrow? It looked like I would walk through Glasgow despite my desire to go around it. Lodging defined my route.

I continued to feel an urgency and unsaid expectations. At some level I felt I had to demonstrate to others that I could make it to Aberdeen. The feeling was lessening but it was much more than necessary. Emotionally I wanted to prove myself. Logically I knew that no one really would think less of me if I only made it to someplace closer like Dundee. On my ride across America I never got past worrying and was continually optimizing. I felt that the trip was unresolved when I only made it to Pensacola instead of Key West. Sometime in the intervening years I'd progressed. I wondered if I would feel the same compulsion for completeness if that happened again.

The sunset colors deepened as I sipped my whisky. The view from the bar was partly obscured by the landscaping and the sea wall. The view from my upstairs room would be much better. They didn't mind if I took the drink upstairs, so I managed to snag a sunset photo by taking the whisky for a walk. Nature's show was better than the BBC. Relaxed barkeeps didn't get in the way of my relaxation.

There was one last task for the evening. The room was equipped with a luxury: a sewing kit. It gave me the opportunity to mend my pants leg. A guardrail ripped it during one of my episodes dodging traffic. I danced with and away from the traffic, but sometimes I stumbled too.

Settling into bed meant shifting most of what was in my pack. As I lay there I couldn't fall asleep. I carried troubles too, and they kept me awake, but the thin walls put my life in perspective. My neighbor was crying. She sobbed in waves that gradually subsided. I was reluctant to do anything in such a reticent and foreign country. I listened for angry knocks on her door in case she needed an ally, but she didn't need me. As long as she was alone she was probably safe. I felt for her and wished her well and stayed in my room.

Storybook Suite

September 27
Prestwick - Fenwick

Rain. Rain and the start of a long day, or maybe a really short one if it rained too much. It was hard to tell. I was getting closer to Glasgow, but it was more than a full day away unless I miraculously manifested a bicycle. Surely the towns will be bigger and closer together as I approached a metropolis, despite what the map showed. If the rain didn't stop early, I might.

There was an airport in my way. The streets converged into a highway that swept around the runway. Prestwick's airport is an active, good-sized airport, with acres of parking lots, lots of sidewalks, advertisements, traffic, and a regular stream of flights.

Every take-off was an opportunity to watch metal leave the Earth and climb into the sky. Even with a degree in aerospace engineering I marveled at the magic. It was entertaining, but the long sweep added a mile or so to my day.

The traffic circles and their signs were a bit confusing. They were designed to steer ticket-holders to the airport, not to direct cross-country pedestrians around the perimeter. Innovative travel results in journeys that cuts across convention and lacks clear signposts. A lot of guessing and trust was involved.

My guess of a route took me past Prestwick's aerospace industry on the far side of the airport. That's an old comfort zone. I wondered what my eighteen years at Boeing would be worth in Scotland. Possibly little. I worked in airplane development. There are very few places on the planet that do that. My perspective changed. Because I spent some time imagining working there I spent some time imagining living there. I scrutinized the neighborhoods. I noticed how many people were walking, bicycling, carpooling, and driving to work. I wished I'd spent more time perusing Prestwick.. Walking through a place isn't as intimate as stopping and staying for years. Tourists' and residents' perspectives rarely coincide.

The morning commute was the same as anywhere. Cars pulled over to pop out commuters. Bicycles and buses streamed in, though only sporadically. I suspect the people I saw were a little late. They hurried. I strolled, and reminded myself that what I really preferred was for my stocks, books, and photos to pay my bills. A life based on investments and art would give me a lot more time for travel and fun. Sufficient passive income would make it easier to relax and enjoy.

The neighborhoods segued from dense to open to rural. Eventually I walked past farmland again, where houses' names were as prominent as their numbers. Back home, if a house has a name, it's probably a bed and breakfast. For a while I thought that there'd be plenty of places to stay, but they were merely signs of pride. Is that why some people thought the countryside was peppered with accommodations? It would be an easy assumption to make while driving by.

I'd learned that asking for directions or advice was best done three times over. Where's the next place to stop? Which way do I go? What time do they open? When I could, I'd ask each traveler's question to three different people. That only happened in towns. Farmland wasn't populated enough. Asking the livestock for directions didn't help or count. Sometimes asking the same person three times had a clarifying result. They'd get fed up after the first two tries and reword it a third time and cover a key point they'd skipped. The same thing happened when I asked myself about me. Why am I doing this? Why am I doing this? Why am I doing this? Because I should. Because I have to. Because some childhood episode engrained in me the belief that doing something similar would bring me gratification and acceptance.

The illusion of introspectively strolling through the vacant countryside was dispelled when a mother with a baby stroller passed me at full speed. No hello or anything, just the sound of hurried footsteps and the rattle of wheels. It was a bit humbling, and then I chuckled at myself when I considered picking up my pace. Relax. Then a businesswoman in a fashionable pants suit powerwalked by me. No hint of sweat or huffing or puffing. Am I really that slow? I thought I was in vacant countryside but it was a buffer zone between the airport and a bedroom community on the next ridge. I hadn't noticed it. Their pace was a bit humbling, but it was also a reminder of the freneticism of daily life. Power on through to the next task and chore without saying hello. The neighborhood looked perfectly situated to be just far enough away from the airport and the factory to minimize noise and assure that most people would have to burn petrol to get to work.

Scotland is a land of ages. Some like the development was new. A lot was old. All along the walk I passed stone structures that must have been more solid and harder to build than any wood building. Ruins hundreds of years old are too numerous to maintain and renovate, and possibly too cumbersome to remove. A few are preserved and somewhat restored as memorials, museums, and tourist magnets, but there are far more left to ivy, storms, and general decay. Tumbled stones would make it hard for anything besides goats and sheep to trim the weeds. Even the stoutest structures fall, though slowly. There are war ruins on war ruins, something that is rarely seen in America. Scotland's war ruins stretch back to Roman times. The stone walls that defined the pastures better than any title agreement dropped enough stones to be useless otherwise, so they required other barriers. Walls paralleled fences that ran beside hedgerows. Generations of thick bushes were the only defense that was self-replicating.

We think about enduring aspects of civilization, and some will point to the pyramids and The Great Wall as examples of persistence, but for every castle cleaned up for admission and a fee there are many more that decayed into rubble. The majority of what we build fades, and the parts that don't are only maintained at great expense. Stone houses looked like they lasted longer, but they also looked harder to fix. Owners of old houses know that square is a fantasy. Walls, floors, and ceilings warp. Agonizing over imperfections is only survivable in new housing developments that only temporarily appear to be immune to degradation. The countryside displayed scattered evidence of attempts at permanence, though long lines of vegetation hid old linear structures, and bushes surrounding chimneys marked housing rabbits where people once lived.

Suburbia reappeared. I came across a restaurant that wasn't open for lunch yet, and that had no advice about where to find lodging, a golf course that was for day-use only from what I could tell, and a mini-strip mall of a nursery, cafe, and bicycle shop. I skipped the food because I was more interested in advice. I wasn't bicycling, but shop owners that sold people-powered transports were probably more aware of pedestrian issues than the clerks in the lunch room. Where could I sleep? How could I get around or through Glasgow? The two dudes inside were setting up shop as if they'd just moved into the space. While one built bikes, the other took the time to chat. I talked about my ride across America. He talked about how risky it was to start a business. But he was encouraging. Evidently the signs I'd seen for a National Bicycle Network were the beginnings of something useful. But they were only the beginnings.

The network wasn't stitched together. It was individual strands that almost pointed to each other. None of them were woven into a pattern that I could use. They also didn't know of any place to stay, which surprised me because Kilmarnock was only a mile or so away and looked like a sizable city. I bought some Clif bars, and they gave me what advice they could: directions to and through the pedestrian part of town, assurances that walking through Glasgow would be fine, and a passing comment as I left that maybe I should avoid one particular neighborhood on the edge of Glasgow. He grew up there. He seemed hesitant. And then they wished me well.

City life was different, or at least it was easier to concentrate on the fresh, the tidy, and the clean. Their directions swept me into the urban density that was Kilmarnock's pedestrian mall. The cobbled pedestrian-only street was a welcome change from walking with cattle. From striding past livestock herds that either fled or followed me to mixing with crowds of shopping pedestrians that ignored and flowed around me was a midday culture shock. At least there wasn't a chance of mud. My boots were out of place. I didn't have to watch my feet. No one did. Urban life paves over many otherwise everyday nuisances.

The shopping district had as many choices as any American mall, including shops that were practical, but the only one I stopped in was the bookstore. Traveling alone for weeks can be lonely, and books are lightweight surrogate companions. As for the rest of the shops, walkers carry everything, and anything I bought would either have to be eaten, left behind, shipped, or carried for days and miles. Food and books, consumables, were the only things on my very short shopping list. Souvenirs were a luxury to be bought the final day. I passed through Kilmarnock without talking to anyone unless a cash register was involved.

There were rumors of other places to stay, and I reminded myself that if I didn't find a bed, at least I could probably find a bus back to Prestwick or up to Glasgow. I used that logic even though I rarely saw a bus. The afternoon was overcast but dry. Rain wanted to return, and it would eventually. In the meantime, I didn't have to squint from the sun or hide under a layer of artificial fabric.

Rural reasserted itself with farmhouses that either shared a wall with the road or were so far back that the driveways were lost behind lines of trees. The farmhouses were quaint, cute, sturdy, pragmatic, every shade of stereotypical reference to simpler times with more basic needs and solutions. The farm buildings were modern and industrial. Wood and stone barns existed, but far more acreage and volume was devoted to sheet metal structures that were characterless and optimized for practicality. Form followed function and function ruled over all, except for the houses. Evidently, quaint rural lives were lived based on habit, but the farms were run based on business principles that had no regard for historical esthetics. Business and money dictate universal concepts of the economy of scale. It wasn't a surprise. The Scots are known for thinking things through.

The clouds dropped and hinted with sprinkles. The town of Fenwick was only a few miles from Kilmarnock, and the spot on the map where my highway went from minor to major. The A highway became an M motorway, which in the UK seemed to be the difference between a US highway and the

Interstate. The A roads had stop lights, and sporadic shoulders and sidewalks. The M roads might have onramps and signs saying "No Pedestrians." I hoped for a side road that would parallel the highway and provide me with a route. Either that or I was walking into a dead end. I hoped a big highway entrance would collect hotels. I'd relied on off-ramp motels on my ride across America. My logistics would be simplified and my worries eased if I could count on such a trend in Scotland, but I hadn't seen any evidence of them.

Fenwick didn't seem to be in a hurry to turn from rural to urban. A few extra houses appeared as I rounded a bend or two. They weren't as interesting as the sign that finally appeared just after my legs ramped up their complaints. The bad news was that the tourism bureau put so many stars beside the name of the hotel that it only took me a minute to decide to move along. Five stars sound nice, but I didn't feel like paying for the last one or two. Besides, I could always learn to backtrack if I didn't find anything else. I hoped for hotels, but maybe Fenwick was too small to have more with one. I'd misguessed tourist services every day. Maybe this time there'd be a better choice just ahead. It was worth my time to explore a little and possibly save the price of at least a star.

Sometimes patience takes years. Sometimes it only takes moments. As I approached a cluster of homes, a B&B sign pointed to what looked like a dead-end lane. Normally I wouldn't have checked it out because there was no hint of a place for dinner, but they looked more affordable, and bigger buildings looked close enough. I took the turn.

Scotland has old houses. This one was built when the others were patches of wilderness. A couple had renovated a farmhouse, Langside, that sprawled organically. The house's arms and wings wrapped gardens and livestock. The walls were freshly painted white stucco bracketed by black iron railings and gates. It looked too good to be true. Maybe good things happen. Besides, 14 miles makes a body ready to stop. I unlatched the gate and knocked on what I guessed was the front door. My grey day brightened when an eager young miss answered with a smile and had a youthful bounce. We were contrasts. She bounced back into the house to get her mother who was equally welcoming but much more refined. Yes, they were pleasantly surprised to have a guest. They weren't expecting anyone, but there was a room available. The price was good enough for me. I was glad I kept walking.

They didn't have a room. They had a suite. For slightly more than what I'd been paying, I got a bedroom as large as my living room and a bathroom larger than my kitchen. The walls were stone, not a facade. The four poster bed looked stout enough for gymnastics. The armoire could hide four. The decor was masculine yet plush. If I found a place this good at the coast with a pub next door I might never have moved, and the entire time I'd be wondering why I was alone in such a romantic setting. My hostess showed me around and then, in classic Scottish frugal style, announced that she'd be in later to turn the heat on. The stone walls were cold and could absorb a lot of heat before the room warmed up. She'd just come in and warm up the air when I needed it. Besides, I was going to spend the rest of the afternoon in town and at the pub, right?

Maybe. I wanted a hot shower. Warmed by the water I didn't want to give up any heat, and I wanted to get off my feet. I snuggled under the covers for a nap.

I relaxed until the 4PM-5PM window. If I was lucky, I could get trail food at a shop before it closed and dinner in the pub after it opened. I didn't want to make two trips. The general store was quite specific. I've been in general stores that outfit farm families. Fenwick's general store was smaller than my suite. At least they had a few energy bars for the next day's walk. A few steps away was the pub. It was right, proper, and a pleasure. It was also part of a chain that sometimes includes rooms: King's Arms. If I'd walked a little farther, I could've stayed above the pub and simply stumbled down the stairs to dinner. But I doubt that the accommodations would have been as sweet as my suite. I grabbed a seat in the corner, by the window, got out my notebook, pen, and map, and didn't hide the fact that I was a tourist. Despite such obvious Scottish offerings like Deep Fried Black Pudding and Haggis Pakora, I had a Steak and Guinness pie with a whisky as dessert. A photo would capture a stereotype, but techno-pop music and posters for country western line dancing brought it back to reality. The dancing wasn't for another month. Maybe I should've walked in October.

My dinner-time map research convinced me that Glasgow was too long of a walk for one day. Seventeen miles was doable, but I'd prefer to stop at my average thirteen. That would leave me shy of the city and its loud and expensive hotels, and position me nicely for popping through the city in a day that would end in quieter and cheaper surroundings on the far side.

Sunset was early enough and the walk into town was long enough that I only wanted to do it once and in the light. I could've gone back for dessert or a night cap, but I wasn't going to chastise myself for not adding that many miles to my day. I walked back in a deepening dusk.

The heat was on, but the air had a chill, so I got under the covers again. Life was opulent. Thick blankets, rich wood, solid stone, and a well-fed me with a good book for a companion. Okay, so maybe one thing could be improved. Books comfort the mind, but my body would've preferred a more romantic companion. I read and relaxed into the most comfortable nest so far.

In bed. Lights out. Looking forward to a good night's sleep. Just as I drifted off the donkey brayed in the dark. Where'd they hide a donkey? I'm not out of the farmlands yet.

I should keep walking. I wanted to stay. What would make me change my mind?

Joy And Torment

September 28
Fenwick - Glasgow

Breakfast was served for one. Their other guest came in after me and was up and gone before 8am. Maybe the donkey brayed when the guest arrived in the night. They sat me at the head of the table like I was the head of the house. Nice house and people. I wouldn't mind.

Over my nettle tea my hostess talked to me about a bicycle trail at the end of their lane. Evidently the lane wasn't a dead end. Evidently she assumed I stopped at her place because I knew about the trail. How else would I have found them? Serendipity happens. The lane and the trail passed under the highway and then followed local roads towards

Glasgow. I was living life right. If I'd followed the main road and stayed at the King's Arms I might have led me to the motorway that was great for cars but was a dead end for pedestrians. By luck I'd stopped at the one house that marked the intersection with the National Bicycle Network.

As I closed the garden gate, I looked down the lane. The morning light made it look like less of a dead-end, but it wasn't very encouraging seeing the path dive into the dark tunnel of the underpass. It looked like an opportunity for Joseph Campbell to begin a lecture on the hero's journey. What lay within and beyond the darkness?

From light, to dark, and back to light as I crossed over to the other side was like a Wizard of Oz moment. The sky was lightly overcast. The contrast was bright and welcome. A regular road roughly paralleled the heavy traffic and steered away from the highway. Soon the road noise drifted away. As a bonus, instead of a sidewalk, shoulder, or bit of paint defining a lane there was a wide concrete median guarding a paved path wide enough for bicycles to ride abreast. I had a mini-road all to myself and a bigger barrier to traffic than I imagined. Fenwick was luxurious.

I also had a lot of country to myself. Instead of finding more density closer to the metropolis of Glasgow, I walked through more farmland. Only seventeen miles from downtown Glasgow is a big emptiness. The motorway sped everyone through the terrain with little effect except noise and exhausts. Credit goes to car companies that the exhausts weren't bad. Thirty years earlier the air was probably much fouler. My route was far enough away that I was more likely to smell the cow fumes instead of car fumes. They both came from tailpipes, but I had a preference.

Congratulations Scots. One of the farms' crops was odor-free: wind. Individual houses had turbines. Forests of titans gathered on the ridges slicing energy from the air. Unlike America, where the wind and the cities can be far apart, in Scotland the turbines were within a twenty minute drive of downtown. The energy didn't have far to go.

The lands rolled up and down. I saw more trout farms than people. A bicyclist startled me, which made me laugh at myself. How inattentive, how relaxed must I be to jump when a person rides by? Maybe he cursed the pedestrian that took up the entire bike lane. Maybe he cheered my obviously long walk. Probably he forgot about me within a mile. I passed through a land without making a mark.

I laughed because I was embarrassed. I'd finally relaxed enough to not worry about what others would think when they saw me. Hours spent surrounded by no one were an opportunity to have those conversations I was rarely brave enough to have in person. They were one-sided conversations, but I talked to people who'd died, people I hadn't seen in years, friends who were also always too busy to sit and talk. Emotions had a chance to arise without someone telling me how I should feel or having to worry about how I should respond. Manners, politeness, diplomacy could all be ignored. I said thank yous to people who usually have to be convinced to take a compliment, or I talked about something that bugged me without having to defend or justify my emotion. They never answered back, I wasn't that tired, but I could pretend that they were listening. The cattle didn't seem to care, and I was less likely to scare the sheep because they had a chance to hear me coming. When the cyclist rolled by I was so deep in my own world that I didn't know if I had been talking out loud. Oh well, rather than worry about my image I decided I could always claim to just be a crazy Yank tourist.

Somewhere in there something else happened. There was a moment that wouldn't show up in a video. I was walking one moment, and was walking the next. Between those moments was a flash of a powerful emotion. I glimpsed joy. For the infinitesimal time between two moments, I somehow opened my self up and met an emotion I thought I knew. After being properly introduced I was humbled by how little I knew about it. Amidst the arguments and expressive outbursts I realized why I was walking across Scotland. Yes, I should take a vacation for my health. Yes, I wanted to get away from my chores for a while. But I suddenly realized that I was walking across Scotland because I could enjoy it. Such a simple thing as walking could be described as mobile meditation or low-impact aerobics or many other multi-syllabic rationalizations - but the real reason I was walking across Scotland was because I enjoyed walking, and travel, and unstructured time, and having a straightforward goal. I was enjoying myself. I saw joy and recognized it in a real sense, and realized that I'd only known it in ideal sense until then. I recognized that joy was in every moment, and that it was always waiting for me. I simply had to choose it. For over fifty years I'd never witnessed the purity of that feeling nor learned that simple truth. I'd done well in school, behaved myself, graduated college with a respectable degree, got a good job, got a better degree, got a better job, saved my money, managed the suburban lifestyle, and ended up single again because I should. Nowhere in there did I spend much time learning to enjoy. I acted responsibly and learned to do the things that people said were enjoyable, and believed that what I experienced was joy. But I was wrong. For one moment, without a break in the clouds, or finding money at my feet, or seeing a beautiful smile, I felt full of joy. I was walking across Scotland because I enjoyed walking across Scotland. There was no need for any greater discussion.

The next moment arrived and the feeling was gone. Yet, a tendril remained. An emotional thread tied me to the awareness that I could have that feeling and the memory of the real instead of the ideal emotion. I tried snapping back into joy, but could tell it didn't work that way. I'd spent so little time experiencing real joy that I would require practice to get that feeling back. Slipping back into familiar feelings was inevitable. Chastising myself for it wouldn't help. I decided to keep a tender mental hold on that emotional thread and slowly reel in that treasure. Within a few minutes I was back to my conversations, but there was a lightness to my face. My jaw and forehead relaxed. I'd turned a corner into a long and eagerly anticipated journey and education.

Hours passed and I slid back into old habits. I began my daily worry about where I'd spend the evening. There weren't many road signs to guide me, or tell me how many more miles, kilometers, or hours to the next town. I'd left the highway behind. If I'd been dropped there without knowing about Glasgow I would've guessed that I was walking towards wilderness.

Eventually signs of civilization showed up: golf courses. Immaculately manicured green lawns can be considered environmental resource sinks and pollution producers, but in Scotland they make sense. This is the land that invented the game, and the courses are natural; or at least the terrain doesn't require as much earthmoving, and the climate makes sure that there isn't as much need for artificial encouragements to make the grass grow. Scottish golf courses looked perfectly positioned and made desert courses look ludicrous.

A nice restaurant marked the turn from rural to suburban. It was situated on its own land with a bit of a buffer between it, the farms, and the developments. As usual, I was there before they opened. Pity. Breakfast had been somewhat light, and I'd already traveled a few miles. I walked in, surprised the hostess, and knew that it would be a long while before they could serve me. Just like everyone else, they gave me car directions and times to other restaurants and places to stay. One hour in a car could cover four days of travel by foot.

Travel challenges expectations. If a trip happens without surprises, it's a scripted itinerary that is academic and passive. If expectations aren't challenged the trip may be more like watching than doing. It's the difference between tuning into the Tour de France versus going out for a bicycle ride. I had expectations, but I expected to be surprised. Food and lodging weren't as frequent as I expected. There were fewer people about. Buses and trains didn't pass by often enough to remind that they were an option. I was okay with that, but having my expectations exceeded would have been a nice variation too.

Golf courses were nice to walk along, but soon they were replaced with parking lots, houses, and fortunately more opportunities for advice. Density hadn't increased gradually as I left Fenwick, so I guessed that some zoning regulation created pockets for pastures and pockets for people. That might mean the step from empty to packed might be as abrupt as stepping past a sign. That didn't happen either. Finally, density began to ramp up and eventually I found a shopping mall wedged into a neighborhood. Shopping malls sound useful but they tend to congregate less-useful businesses. Fashionable clothes and cosmetics weren't what I needed. I needed directions for getting through or around Glasgow, and useful suggestions for a place to stay.

Another bicycle shop appeared, not in the core of the mall, but along its periphery. Back at the restaurant outside of town they thought there might be a place in two more miles. I'd walked a nice chunk of that. The customers and the clerks in the bike shop thought I had about two more miles to go. They made it sound easy to find so I didn't ask for a lot of details. Besides, we spent more time talking about my ride across America. Their shop was called Adrenaline, but the irony was that my bike ride, my hikes, my walks are endurance feats. Adrenaline rarely arises.

As I walked out of the mall I realized that I'd forgotten to buy lunch. A take-away shop down the street had deep-fried fast food sitting under heat lamps. They had something new to me, a deep-fried hamburger. How did American fast food miss the possibility of the deep-fried beef patty? Culinary experiments are fun, but I also wanted to make sure I'd have familiar fuel; so, I bought an order of fish and chips too. My hands were full of food. I had a hot, greasy, walking feast. It was the sort of food that is best when hot and slimy when cold. I had great incentives to eat quickly. Besides, the quicker I ate the sooner I didn't have to juggle lunch. The burger was first. My first bite was pink, runny, and underdone. I stared at it, thought about what would happen if it suddenly made a toilet necessary, and decided it was better to put the possibly underdone meat into the trash instead of into me. I was glad for the fish.

The world became decidedly urban. Houses and shops were close enough that pavement was more common than lawn. My speed picked up because I no longer danced along highway shoulders and guardrails or juggling food. The only things I had to avoid were litter and cracks in the sidewalk. The road broadened enough for turn lanes to squeeze into the middle of the road. There were even traffic lights and Walk signs. There were more people to encounter but, in true urban fashion, few of them made eye contact. Protective bubbles of ear wear removed everyone from the person beside them. Bus stops were huddles of people staring up, down, far away, or inside their eyelids. I felt like the only person who was watching the world.

The farther I went the more interested I was in how much farther I had to go. People were so reticent when I asked for directions that I rarely asked. Their answers were short and usually included a guess that there was probably a place a couple miles farther. A couple of miles crossed a lot of storefronts. I expected a lot more opportunities than they described, but then I also knew that locals have little need for extra lodging. They may not be aware of a quiet B&B on their street.

It turned out that they knew what they were talking about. Miles passed. My legs were tiring. The weather was settling into greyer and wetter.

A patch of open land, maybe a large park, broke up the walk for a while. I acknowledged the park but didn't enjoy it because I didn't want to miss any signs. At an intersection with what looked like a motorway on-ramp there was a building that looked like a hotel. Finally, something that fit my world view of hotels and motels at highway interchanges. Looks weren't good enough. I was wrong. It was either condos or apartments and I had to keep walking.

The road took a long swing around the building. My optimism drew my eyes along, hoping for a sign around the curved retaining wall. Reinforcing my optimism was emotionally draining. The road climbed a bit and leveled to reveal a long view with little hope. I fell back into a steady tread, eating up distance, not absorbing the world. I was too busy mentally rummaging around for internal support. Buses went by and I considered them, but I had no idea of how to use them. Did I need tokens? A card? Riding the buses back home on Whidbey was free. I doubted that I'd find such simple service after what I paid for the ride from the airport.

Rows of houses lived behind long brick walls that bordered the sidewalk. The walls and the road created a brick and asphalt trough that constrained me and traffic like water through an irrigation ditch. There was little choice about where I was going. The side streets provided possibilities, but they were also opportunities to get lost or miss useful landmarks.

A small cluster of shops appeared with a few weather-hardy Scots sitting at a sidewalk cafe. I was tired enough that I couldn't tell if I was polite or not. I interrupted their conversation because I needed help. They knew of two hotels, but couldn't remember if either was open. The closest one had the most complicated directions, was less likely to still be in business, and was blocks away from the route. The other was another mile or two along my route, but they knew less about it. Close sounded good, but getting lost sounded bad. Walking farther wasn't appealing, but it was in the right direction, and maybe I'd find something else along the way. I thanked them and continued.

Sprinkles fell, not enough to make me switch into rain gear, especially when I could be checking into a hotel within a half-hour, but enough that I noticed the threat. Hypothermia doesn't only happen in the mountains.

Blocks later there it was, shining in bright white paint on the corner, a tidy old hotel. Quaint and classic, convenient and welcome, and with a lot of stars on its sign. I didn't care about the price. I wanted to lay down. I walked into a small lobby, noticed a lot of suits and dresses that clashed with my walker's wear, and was pleased to see a clerk pop up. He was pleasant. They were full. A wedding booked the entire place. He was sympathetic, but Glasgow wasn't far. Oh, I was walking? Well, there was a place he remembered along my route, but he thought they might have gone out of business. They were about two miles farther. I groaned.

My feet ached. My legs were tired enough that simple mistakes hurt. I stubbed my toe trying to avoid a curb that was a half-step closer than a full stride. Every other step became a pained reminder of the consequence of a momentary lack of confidence. There was no grassy shoulder as a soft alternative or to break the monotony. I was in pavement country. The urban world was unyielding. Trees and shrubs were surrounded by ceramic or concrete pots. Grass was sequestered to a manicured life with sharp edged borders. At least I didn't have to worry about traffic. It was constrained too, though evidently it was alright to park on the sidewalk.

Neighborhoods changed and I walked through one that had its own version of harshness. Houses weren't as well kept. Walls were sootier. The line of cars parked over the curb was almost continuous. There was less room between the houses. Density was definitely increasing. My anxiety increased too. It did not look like the part of town where travelers purposely paid to stay.

Two more miles must have passed, or at least it felt that way, but I hadn't found a hotel. I did see a sign that said, "Welcome to Glasgow" "Please drive carefully". Without intending to I'd reached a goal. Perseverance pays, even when I was aimed at a nearer goal. Oh well, I welcomed myself to Glasgow and decided to walk carefully. My stubbed toe wouldn't let me walk any other way. Stopping short or maneuvering around the city were no longer options.

The skies darkened. Sprinkles increased, but still not enough to warrant rain gear. Pedestrian traffic increased too, but the reticence remained. Gaps between buildings vanished as well as the front yards and driveways. The buildings bordered the sidewalk and added enough floors to dim the lighting by shrinking the sky. There was no longer the hint of sub- associated with -urban.

In the midst of continuous storefronts and ever-present crowds I decided to ask for directions again. Along a rural road there were few choices and hotels were very likely to be along my route. Hotels in cities could be anywhere. Two older women stood at a corner chatting. I interrupted, hopefully politely, explained that I was walking across Scotland, and asked again for directions and advice. They told me about a place called King's Park. There were hotels on the far edge of it. It was only about two miles away. I laughed and thanked them. Two more miles. Two more miles. Two more miles. There'd been too many two more miles. Each two were harder to do. They also delivered a spot of encouragement by describing King's Park as a much nicer neighborhood.

I watched for their landmarks and ignored the rest. I was tired enough that much of it was out of focus. I was walking, not touring.

Eventually a long line of trees arrived and looked like a park. Maybe it was a King's Park. Who else could afford that much space for trees that old in the middle of an historic city?

Here's the park. Where're the signs? There had to be signs. Not at first glance. I slowed and turned in a circle, but couldn't see evidence of Rooms, or Vacancy, or Front Desk This Way. My remaining optimism withered. Any mental buttressing collapsed. At the far edge of the park, where the hotels were supposed to be, I met an old-fashioned street cleaner with his broom and pan in hand. Was there a hotel near here? He was relaxed enough to be Southern. He leaned on his broom, got quiet for a bit, told me he was familiar with the neighborhood but he couldn't remember any hotels within the last few decades. The good news was that there another hotel, but it was about two miles farther. He was sure of it. I managed to slump even more. There probably wasn't a straightened joint in my body.

I'd been walking for six hours without much of a break, into an increasingly dismal day, with a bubble of hope that continually squirted out of reach whenever I almost touched it. It felt like I was already miles inside the city limits. Random chance should be enough to help me find a place within a city as large as Glasgow. I straightened a bit and started walking again.

The city turned from stores and housing into industrial neighborhoods with more graffiti and utilitarian businesses like car shops. Open space appeared for parking lots and then from buildings that were torn down. It was reminiscent of gaps in the forests where the only light touching the ground comes from gaps in the canopy caused by the fall and crash of unlucky trees. Construction and highway interchanges opened the airspace, filled it with noise, and wrapped it in chain link fencing that captured litter. My view was dreary because I was weary.

My body began to rebel. The chest pains from Cairnryan's heart attack hill returned. My back reminded me of our decades-long debate. My head and belly ached. My foot hurt.

Seeing some fine arts building go by was less an encouragement than evidence that someone had force-fit culture into a neighborhood that couldn't afford the ticket. Maybe it all looked better on a sunny day or from within a better mood.

That's when it started to rain. The sprinkles relinquished their reserves in a no-argument rain storm. The sidewalks started to clear. I pulled out my gear and maneuvered around closed sidewalks and detours through construction sites.

Less than a mile later truly modern buildings replaced jumbles of rubble and building supplies.

Steel, concrete, and glass replaced stone architecture. Bright red signs announced unfamiliar brand names. Jury's Inn was the biggest, the reddest, or at least the one that caught my attention. I hoped it wasn't another apartment building or set of condominiums.

It was, however, across a bridge. I hadn't expected a bridge. I hadn't expected to cross any rivers, but the sign said The River Clyde. That sounded familiar without even checking the map. I was in the center of downtown Glasgow. Across the bridge was the core of the metropolis. Beside the bridge that carried me was the bridge that carried the trains. The Jury's Inn shared a wall with the Glasgow train station that I'd left from days ago. It took a six day walk to rewind a few hour train ride. The bridge would've been a place to linger except for the rain and the preceding too many miles.

Across the bridge and on my side of the street was something that was probably far more affordable than the Jury's Inn. Its sign and building were smaller and somewhere on the wall was the word hostel. As I walked past it a trio of elderly bicyclists rode up in wet touring gear. Logically I should have walked in and found what they had to offer because I knew it would cost less than the monument of a hotel across the street. But, I know me. When I get tired enough I want minimal complications and price becomes less of an issue. My choices were one overpriced hotel that probably had much more than I needed, or a minimalist alternative that may fall shy of something that my depleted resources definitely needed. From the outside I could only guess, and I knew I only had enough energy to check in once and collapse. I didn't have the energy to shop. My head, my physical heart, my back and my feet were in need of pampering. I wanted and needed to treat myself. It wasn't a question of indulgence or luxury. I was hurting and didn't have the energy to suddenly become resourceful. I wanted it all with room service.

I crossed the street to the Jury's Inn and hoped they didn't have a dress code. Bedraggled me looked out of place in their lobby. Contemporary luxury was obvious in expanses of wood, expensive and subtle lighting, clerks in uniforms, purposely innocuous music - all the features of a high-end business hotel that thrives on expense accounts. As I walked up to the counter I wondered if they would personally appreciate a break from their routine clientele, or if I was an unwelcome bit of grit in a well-oiled machine. They were nice enough to tell me that the going room rate was 250 pounds. I hesitated. My wallet squeaked. I rummaged around internally again for enough energy to walk out, but decided to appeal to their compassion for a wet, tired and exhausted traveler. They dropped the rate into the high double digits, gave me my room key, and reminded me to call if I had any questions. The rest was a blur. I had a key. I had a room to sleep in on a wet night. And I was in Glasgow.

An elevator, the first I'd been on in Scotland, took me to a room that overlooked the river, the bridge, the train tracks, and the rain. After following their instructions for how to turn on the power (put the room key in the slot on the wall) and using the bathroom, I stripped and collapsed onto the bed. There is a progression from tired to exhausted to stressed. A heart attack would not have been a surprise. I was dizzy and had trouble thinking straight, so I lay there and tried to think of nothing. I was in the midst of a crisis of confidence even though

I'd accomplished miles of travel. Hearing the trains shuttle in and out reminded me of how much effort I'd expended to do so little. It was either the best time to have someone along to pick up my spirits, or the best time to be alone so no one had to suffer my mood. Of course, anyone who'd walked along with me may have felt the same - after we gave each other a hug or a high-five.

Walking alone had its advantages. I could sing as if no one was listening. I could talk as if someone was there. It was a good practice to shelve as I walked through the city. As I laid there, I kept my conversations to myself instead of upsetting the neighbors.

Eventually my heart throttled back to normal and I regained enough power to shower, get into dry clothes, and head to dinner. In less than a week I was already looking forward to my indulgent American shower back home.

A pub would've been great, but convenience was wonderful so I sat down to dinner in their expensive restaurant. The steak came with fries. My mood improved. All it needed was a bit of rest and a lot of food. My body and brain were fueled again. The whisky didn't hurt. Some may be able to exercise mind over matter, but when I'm hungry I get grumpy; especially when hours of two more miles are involved.

The indulgence felt good. I sat by the windows and watched other travelers walk into the hostel. I probably would've been fine there too. But I wasn't going to apologize for the occasional luxury, especially when I could be celebrating. A cruise, a beach resort, diving into Las Vegas would all be indulgences too, but most vacations are static. A body sits and spectates and maybe shops and definitely eats and drinks. I've been to Jamaica. I've been to Vegas. Walking felt better. The simple act of walking gave my mind and body just enough to occupy them without taxing them, except when I occasionally pushed too far. Sitting lets my mind either drift, which is good; or swirl, which is bad. Three weeks on the beach, even with a stack of excellent books, might have given me too much time to worry. Playing in the water is fun exercise, but it can only be done for a few hours a day, and it didn't seem to fit my mood. I wanted some sense of accomplishment, and walking was equipped with a new goal and new views every day. Every day I passed a new horizon and saw a new world.

What would be a more perfect, indulgent vacation? What did I want? Totally decadent travel would be with people I loved, in good weather, with someone else carrying our gear, along a route that was easy to follow, through countryside that was pleasant, and ending each day with a good place to eat and stay. Hiring the right guide and getting lucky with the weather could accomplish that, and probably cost a lot less than exotic cruises.

I enjoy walking the world. Between the tourist attractions is a real world that isn't sanitized or overly ordered. Variations from the norm interest me. I was delivering days of interesting life to myself.

Business travelers were scattered, one to a table. I lived that life when I was an engineer. Solitary enclaves of recuperation or preparation between business deals, presentations, and assignments fill an empty space with maximum room between each diner. I sat there, enjoying a Guinness, and writing notes. Maybe they thought I was working too. The staff may have thought I was some traveling food critic. Well, that's one way to get better service.

The over-used computer in the lobby was a tie to home. Emails were read and replied. I posted my progress for the curious and so folks didn't worry.

I felt human as I went back to my room. Early to bed was a non-negotiable command.

Water Above Below And Everywhere

September 29
Glasgow - Kirkintilloch

Oh, please let me sleep in. I was talking to myself, but myself wasn't listening. I really wanted to take a day off and let my body rest, especially after such a prolonged version of "two more miles." The view through my window was warped by the sheet of water from the unrelenting rain. Yesterday's afternoon rain was only sprinkles compared to the morning's drenching. There were plenty of reasons to stay, but one big reason to move. The room cost too much. I wasn't going to sit still in a such a high-priced hotel. At half the price and with a good bookstore and pub, I might stay a day, but finances and a desire for greener surroundings moved me along.

I joined the busy businessmen at the breakfast buffet. The shuffling lines, the heat lamps, the sneeze guards, the steam trays, the arms reaching through for pardon me just one thing, the small groups quickly planning for an early meeting were all familiar from my engineering days. It was the first day of something different from breakfast, but it was over quickly and wasn't memorable. Soon I clomped my hiking boots across the pristine lobby floor and out the door.

My pack was lighter because all of the rain gear was out of it and on me. As I stepped outside I checked the time. It was early. The freneticism inside had me eat one of my largest breakfasts in the least time. The cost and pace of a pricy hotel pushed me into urban chaos and stress after a day of exhaustion. I looked forward to a day off. I wanted a day off. I'd look for it somewhere else.

The weather was the same as when I flew in. Maybe it always rains in Glasgow. Pedestrians hurried, but they moved as if rain was the norm. It was like a rainy day in downtown Seattle. In drizzle, people stroll. In rain, they're more likely to pick up the pace if they're dressed fashionably, or demonstrably slowly if they were proudly wearing rain clothes. Few dash, and fewer linger. I unfashionably ambled. Moving faster wouldn't make me drier and I expected to be walking through the weather for hours.

I also didn't take many pictures. The only dry place for my camera to come out was in the rain shadow of a building that spanned a street.

A chaos percolated within my head. A city has too many choices. All along the coast, the morning's route started with a clear direction. Follow the coast or flow down the funnel of roads that ended at the center of Glasgow. Landmarks in the country are singular buildings or occasional roads. Glasgow has a grid stamped into its inner street pattern, but the roads leading into the country broke free and followed routes that were probably centuries old. Looking down a road didn't give me a hint of where it might end. All I knew was that I was heading generally north of Edinburgh. I hadn't decided about which side of the Firth of Forth to follow. One day at a time. The directions I gleaned from my map and the drenched pedestrians led me to landmarks that were campuses sprawled across blocks instead of singular buildings. As targets they had no definite edge, so standing in the middle of one might not give me a clue about where to find the next road. I had a compass, but it was electronic and confused. Its guesses bounced about as if I was on a boat.

There's a karate strategy that says, "Don't move unless it is to your advantage." But I was on a journey and standing still wasn't to my advantage either. When in doubt I walked.

Downtown offices were left behind. The architecture became more modern with brick instead of stone and then concrete replacing brick. And then concrete leapt into the sky as a curls of onramps, overpasses, and walkways. Each asymptoted to a direction but usually only after it was out of sight. I stared up at concrete and into the rain trying to read highway signs aligned for drivers' views. I wasn't worried, but I wondered if I'd spend more time thinking than walking, more time hunting for signs than making progress.

Angels exist. Either that or stereotypes are determined to be sustained. Who better to lead a single confused Yank than a young lass with curly red hair flowing past her shoulders, a freckled face, friendly green eyes, a captivating smile, and an entrancing accent? I found her in a courtyard of trees and older buildings by looking confused and lost. She took the time to listen to my vague goal and then confidently gave me directions. I tried to memorize them but I was distracted by her looks, internal jokes about doubting stereotypes, and the wonder at how her hair stayed that pristine in a downpour. She wished me well and vanished. I stood there trying to line up her directions with the landmarks around me. Maybe I should have had her point instead of just talk because I remained a bit confused. But I was grinning in the rain.

I've become more comfortable trusting the universe. Whether real, imagined, or rationalized, frequently I find hints, suggestions, and help when I need it. He who looks for luck finds it. The total amount of luck may be the same, but some are looking and some are not. Whether that is true or not, I was glad that sometimes help showed up in such an appealing fashion.

At least at times like that I know I am human because I remembered her looks more than her directions. But she had inspired a general direction and notes about a few routes to avoid and I trusted my intuition to fill in the gaps. A few minutes later I was past the tangle of concrete, and any tangle within my head, and walking past mass produced economy apartment buildings.

The sidewalk and path were bordered by a motorway set in a concrete trough and fringed with metal fencing. It looked like a neighborhood to walk through and not loiter in. Scotland was reasonably clean, but maybe the rain and my doubts heightened my awareness of the graffiti and trash. The environment had changed and so had the people. My whimsical angel at the edge of a campus was replaced with people bundled, huddled, and scurrying through the rain.

Confidence was hard to find. I knew I was heading out of Glasgow but I didn't know if I was on a path that would take me northeast. Pedestrian trails, walkways, and routes are frequently designed by advocates of recreation who want to entice healthy living by steering people through pleasant surroundings or away from the unpleasant alternatives. Destinations are secondary. I followed a path that followed the highway, except when it didn't. Each deviation at an intersection was an opportunity for an undesired tour of a neighborhood or small shopping district. My fears were based on my history. Unsigned recreational trails that led to great views are impressive and useless to a traveler. I wanted to walk to Aberdeen, not visit an apartment complex.

As Glasgow retreated, the trail narrowed. The buildings shrunk to a story or two. Businesses became more utilitarian. Auto shops replaced clothing boutiques. A precinct house was obviously authoritarian, stout, and functional, but it was a less intimidating size. Side trails led to parking lots and dead ends.

The rain dampened everything. My rain gear was essential. The few without a coat or hat either walked very slowly resigned to their condition, or scurried trying to move as quickly as possible without splashing through puddles. My camera stayed covered. I didn't mind skipping a visual record of the day's walk. Besides, without a record, my selective amnesia could edit my memories. They'd become a preferred fiction rather than an undeniable fact.

A motorway followed a line close to the diagonal I preferred, but the road I found steered north and away. I was carrying a country map, not a city map, so the area around Glasgow wasn't detailed enough to distinguish side roads that paralleled major arteries. Maybe I missed a quicker route to the head of the Firth of Forth. Back in Glasgow I'd realized that to get to Scotland's northeast corner I could either aim east for Edinburgh and hope for a pedestrian friendly bridge across the Firth, aim a bit more northerly and find a narrower Firth and a shorter bridge, or aim inland near Stirling and avoid the Firth entirely. My free tourist map of the country had a dot marked Kirkintilloch that was off the motorway but somewhat along a line I could sketch between Glasgow and Dundee. A city marked by a dot should have a hotel, right?

Rugged Scotland is pinched. I'd sketched a route of hundreds of miles from Stranraer to Aberdeen to commemorate crossing my country on my bicycle. This was the time to remember the cheater's route. The country is almost split by the Firth of Clyde that cuts in from the west to Glasgow and the Firth of Forth that cuts in from the east to Stirling. A walk from Glasgow to Stirling bisects the country in about thirty miles, two days walk or a run slightly longer than a marathon.

I don't cheat, but I do keep my options in mind. Declare success by achieving the simplest goal. That rarely feels gratifying. Even reaching Pensacola, Florida after riding from north of Seattle didn't feel complete. Three thousand miles weren't enough. I wasn't emotionally satisfied until I'd reached Key West. I'd know I'd reached a good enough goal after I had a complete story with a beginning, a middle, and an end with a few anecdotes thrown in. Then I could settle into some town that was quiet, cheap, had a good view, enough books, and a good pub. I also knew that it was personal. Audiences are gracious and accept whatever goal goes with the story. Retelling grand adventures are compressed to an hour at an event, and a few minutes at a party. The goal was more important to me. Listeners would care more about the stories. Something in me felt that I should bring home a string of tales, but I knew that the internal feeling of completion was more important. I could publicly celebrate a completed story as long as I eventually ended up seeing salt water on my right.

The rain kept my head down. My rain hat collected the drops along the brim where they'd hang in front of me, waiting to fall. I shook them off every few minutes. The further I dipped my head, the easier they were to shake off, the more I was protected from the wind, and the less I saw. I sacrificed the view for comfort. Miles passed with me gazing at the sidewalk, with occasional glances up to look ahead for puddles and traffic. Somewhere in there the city stepped back and left me in the midst of fields edged with trees.

The land flattened. The constant rain created puddles along the shoulders and filled the gutters beside the sidewalks. Irrigation or drainage ditches were filled and shot fire hoses of water through culverts under the road. My rain gear was tested, and mostly passed, but it didn't get an A. My solid leather hiking boots gradually absorbed water. A sign welcomed me to the canal district.

A canal district? I hadn't heard about a canal district, but it made sense and the Scots are very sensible people. Evidently, hundreds of years ago, canals were cut between the coasts. The island wasn't cut in two by glaciers, but it is now bisected by water. If it was flat there'd be no locks, but hills exist so locks were added to lift and drop the boats. Between each lock was flat land tied to the next step up or down by small slopes or short staircases. Without any research or planning I stumbled upon a sweet, flat, picturesque and useful path. I didn't know it until I started to see the signs. Happy surprises happen.

When I was brave enough to look around I was treated to artistic views. Rain raises color contrasts. Rose hips and leaves were deep red and green. Any dusty still life was washed with revitalized colors. The views were shortened by low clouds and water in the air, which cropped the landscape into subtle vignettes within moving frames of misty white. Close-ups were easier to focus on, like the composition of ivy draped across an old low stone wall. There were longer, more subtle views but the closer ones were easier to look at as I kept my head down. My horizons were defined by my hat's brim. I couldn't see past my personal defense against the conditions.

I wanted a break and, aside from the terrain, the world wasn't encouraging me to walk farther. The cold, wind and rain thrown at me convinced me to stop early, if it was possible. Evidence of a town appeared. Houses were closer to the road. Sidewalks became a line instead of a series of dashes. Bus stops popped up. When I bicycled across America, towns announced themselves with water towers. In Scotland I looked for steeples. In my fantasy world, the road would head to the steeple, bisect the center of town, and carry me to lots of pubs and hotels. The first steeple was off to the right by blocks or a large chunk of a mile. Road signs pointed to attractions off to the right. The weight of suburbia was off to the right. Off to the right looked like a maze of streets and a lot of possibilities and a lot of unknowns.

Ask the same question three times and a good answer will probably show up. A couple of dogwalkers, some folks at a bus stop, and a hurried businessman all generally pointed straight ahead, not to the right. They all told me to go up a hill, and only a bit to the right to find to a hotel. I was impressed considering the rain and the earlier reticence. Maybe conditions made a difference. Rain inspired sympathy and compassion. The businessman on the first day, the red-headed angel from the morning, and the kind folk of the afternoon were all helpful and all wet. They weren't pointing me towards the first steeple I'd seen. Go up a few blocks, bear right straight through town, take a left before a church, and a block or two from the motorway is a hotel. Up a hill, and how steep and high is the hill? Across town, and how wide is the town? And how many churches are there, and how far away is the motorway? The hill was steep, but it only felt that way because of the rain and having to wade up the stream of runoff.

The town was Kirkintilloch, which is a city by most standards, and the center was wide enough to enclose every shop I might want, including a bookstore that I intended to visit when I was dry. I thought I found the right church, and I thought I found the signs to the motorway, and eventually I was right, though I had to ask for directions a few more times and walk around the wrong block or two.

It was barely past noon and I was done, as long as the hotel had rooms and would let me in early and in my soggy condition. Please have a room for a wet and weary traveler. The woman sitting behind the front desk stifled a laugh when I tried to check in without messing up the small lobby. With my feet on the doorsill I opened the door, leaned in holding the handle, and asked if they had a room available for an early, compassionate admission. She said yes. Without moving I asked if it would be a good idea if I left the wettest stuff outside while I checked in. She was glad that she didn't have to ask. Most of my outer shell became a pile beside the door. Even without my jacket, hat, and backpack, something managed to drip onto her counter as I looked down to fill out the registration form. My beard wasn't exactly dry, and I couldn't leave it outside.

The hotel was recently refurbished to what I considered to be Euro-upscale. The room was laid out as compactly and efficiently as the cabin on a sailboat. I stripped and hung things from every available hook, plumbing fixture, and window. There was barely enough room left for me to lay down.

Evidently, my pack wasn't waterproof. Everything had absorbed at least some water except my notepad and books. There was a puddle in the top pouch. Every bit of clothing was wet at least somewhere. A few of the drips were in embarrassing places. They'd have to dry before I could head out to resupply myself with books and food. I took a shower to change from being wet and cold to wet and warm, then laid down for a nap. I'd crossed about one degree of latitude and longitude, progress noticeable on a globe.

The second photo from the day was of the view through the rain-streaked window looking down on the walled curve of the motorway. The camera has survived partly because I left it in its case all day.

There wasn't much to do except be grateful for walls, roof, windows, heat, and a bed. There was a gap in the rain, so I made a quick trip outside by changing into the least wet clothes. My chores made me wonder how much farther I could've gone. A bit of a rest put some energy back into my step. But I'd walked every day for a week, so taking an afternoon off was easy and probably necessary.

Regardless of the opportunity to celebrate making it to and through Glasgow, the time between walking and sleeping felt empty without a companion. Some might drink the time away. Others with stouter legs might wander more through town. Folks with considerable wealth could shop and ship, but even when I had considerable wealth my minimalist nature would rather look and appreciate than purchase and store. It was the best time to have a companion. Enthusiasm for playing would be easier. Conversations wouldn't be limited to a few sentences of small talk with strangers. Another pair of eyes would see much more. At least books stood in as surrogate companions who carried on excellent one-sided conversations.

My mood improved because I ran an experiment. I'd feel a smile on my face, not be sure where it came from, and rather than doubt it and turn it off, I'd smile for the sake of smiling. A smile could turn into a chuckle and a laugh and, as long as I stopped before hysteria, I'd found that I'd enjoyed a bit more of the day. The feeling was so new though that as it faded I watched to see where it went. I wanted to find its home so I could visit it more often. It was sad to realize that the feeling was uncommon and unfamiliar. Life shouldn't be so dismal. Pondering all afternoon would probably drive me to drink, and drinking alone in an empty pub didn't appeal to me. I let my subconscious ruminate while the part of me that was awake settled into a cycle of reading and napping.

My clothes were drying but not completely dry. Fortunately, slightly damp pants weren't an issue in the mostly empty hotel restaurant. I was early, which was not a surprise. Drinking my way through the afternoon wasn't appealing, but an early dinner sounded great. I had my first dark beer that wasn't a Guinness. A week of wandering held little liquid diversity. The restaurant was a squared ring: bar along one side and tables surrounding a sunken dance floor. Is there a dance partner around here? Nope, at least not an obvious one. The decor and the lighting were a late afternoon mismatch: dark wood and glare through the windows as the sun broke through. The music was familiar. It was American pop more current than my tastes, but it had a beat and I could dance to it, but not alone. I like couple dancing, lead and follow, swinging and waltzing. For the length of one meal I didn't feel that I was in Scotland anymore, and wasn't sure how I felt about that.

Kirkintilloch claimed to be the Canal Capitol. Canals are flat. Flat sounded good. Flat isn't the same as straight, but if the canals led to the sea they were headed in the right direction for me. Once upon a time, canals were the equivalent of highways. A flat highway wandering between Glasgow and Edinburgh lined with pubs and inns sounded appealing. Routes aren't only optimized for time, distance or effort. Views and amenities can factor in too. Fun is valuable.

I went to sleep hoping to follow canals in the morning, but without a map or any advice, and barely a clue about what I would do. And that was okay.

Sweet Canal

September 30
Kirkintilloch - Denny

Water hung in the morning air, which was
better than it falling as rain. The world was wet
enough that stone walls were dark and wet. Fog hid
signs of modern distractions. The highway hum was
muted with occasional rumbles of truck tire noise on
wet asphalt. The sounds shifted with the light winds.
Kirkintilloch seemed like a modern Brigadoon
keeping the modern world at a distance.

I put on my driest clothes, packed my mostly
dry gear, stepped into boots that were slightly damp,
and headed out to find breakfast and a route. The
forecast was for four more days of rain. Ah, Scotland
in the fall.

The food I found before 10AM was a bar that cranked up the lights to wake up the customers. It was doing a brisk business. The menu was larger than normal, but the selection was slim.

Hunting for food helped me stumble across the highway entrance and a staircase down to a canal. Serendipity had teamed up with hunger to steer me to an appealing route. The canal presented me with two options. I chose left because that was north and so was Aberdeen. Route planning doesn't have to be complicated.

Either the fog lifted, or I walked out from under it. Damp air was effective at pulling warmth out of my body. A shiver and walking warmed me as I passed through shadowed light down the steps to the canal. The tow path was paved and maintained as a park. The air was still. Around a bend to the right, sunshine brightened trees. The light was a strong hint that the canal pointed east for a while.

Within an hour the fog vanished. Bicycling commuters splashed puddles. Runners exercised. A few strollers pushed by. I walked like a diesel, slowly at first, and then steadily. I was passed more than I passed. Within the first mile or so the pedestrian traffic thinned and the road noise faded. I was the noisiest thing on the planet. Even the wind and birds were subdued. Canal water barely flows so it was as quiet as a sheltered lake. My walk was peaceful.

The plants weren't hiding the fact that it was autumn. Trees shed leaves. Wetland grasses and rushes were gold strokes of color across the landscape. The canal, the foliage, the path, and then the trees swept parallel curves towards a perspective point that might be lost behind a bend or interrupted by a bridge. Of course there were swans gliding through. They would be trite in a movie, but they were real and in their place. Finally I found the perfect walk. For hours I strolled without hills or traffic. There weren't many locks. The canals were constructed as flat as possible even if it meant cutting them along a hillside. I was beside a waterway while also looking into a valley. The previous day's rains cleared the air making the views sharp and unimpeded. As the sun shone past the trees, and really as the earth rolled around under the sun, I peeled and packed layers until I was ready to walk in t-shirt weather.

For a long while I walked alone, content, and unencumbered by choices or concerns. I'd follow the path I was on with few choices and fewer worries.

Wondering is easy while wandering, and while that sounds like silly and overly simple word play, it is the sort of random phrase that strolled through my brain. A writer's brain on vacation will have such moments, but I suspect that most writers are too embarrassed to mention them. The slowly changing scenery constantly delivered inspirations, surprises, and insights. That stereotypical beach trip that I should have been on looked less appealing every day. My view changed every few feet. A tree set beside a wild rose set beside a volunteered bulb set beside a bit of old masonry were four views on the world. Different ages and origins told different stories. The natural growth was a reminder of what can happen even without a plan. The flower gone wild was a reminder that fragile beauty can live outside protected confines. The masonry was a reminder of what we can build and the impermanence of everything. My life, or at least my body, is impermanent, can survive outside of perfect security, and will continue with or without a plan. A few feet of trail provided a microcosm of my life and my walk.

Far from town meant few people. Most of them rode or ran by with a quick traffic shout, and they'd be gone. I frequently was in the middle of the lane after minutes of traffic-less progress. It was probably the puddles that moved me to the middle. I'll blame it on them.

One man broke the mold that defined Scots as extroverts indoors and introverts outdoors. He rode up on his bike, and instead of steering around me and continuing towards the next town, he said hello and rolled along at my pace for a while. When he realized I was from the States and heard about my journey he asked if he could walk along with me for a while. He is a Scot, divorced a year earlier, pined for his ex-wife, and felt out of place in Scotland. He loved the country, but everyone in the pub knew his story and weren't as supportive as he needed. They'd heard the story enough times already. He had traveled to other continents to work in various mining communities. He missed the Western Hemisphere and its more relaxed attitudes. I had an image of pubs as neighborly. He missed the relaxed anonymity of American bars. Maybe it's just that the beer is always better in the other guy's tavern. Our talk lasted less than a mile though. He was out for a break and some exercise. When we got to a road crossing, we shook hands. I continued and he turned around to peddle home. I hoped he'd find someone to hear his story, or find that he found a new and better story.

Walking with someone is fun. I have friends I can walk with and talk with for hours. I enjoy those walks and miss them when responsibilities get in the way. Walking with someone is also distracting. Being distracted is a great way to make lots of progress while ignoring aches and fatigue. When I'm talking I'm less likely to be conducting bodily system checks. A companion changes the stories too. On the downside, two friends wrapped up in a conversation may never notice a hawk sitting in a tree overhead. On the upside a second set of senses might notice something that the first set missed. How many pubs did I miss because I overlooked a sign?

Walking alone is more meditative and introspective. I was freer to do what I wanted, but I was also more likely to get lost in my thoughts and miss bits of the world. Replaying a childhood episode from a new vantage point could draw me in, while my feet carried me along like a horse heading to the barn. Minutes later I'd look up, bring my eyes level, and find that my feet had transported myself to some new part of the world. Looking back would refresh the barest of memories of passing a stoic house or a pleasant pasture. It is impossible to see it all. Whether alone or not, much of the world goes by unnoticed. I passed horizons without a thought, or because I thought too much.

I passed through towns. My map had dots suggesting possibilities, but except for Twechar, the towns seemed to have drifted away from the canal and berthed themselves to the highway. Maybe there was lodging, but the few times I found anyone to ask, they usually pointed over the hill or around a bend and uncertainly suggested possibilities. No one really knew.

Serendipity happens and I am easily entertained. I got to a lock at the same time as a boat. Operating the lock probably hadn't changed much in hundreds of years, except for the clothing. His fluorescent high-visibility jacket was a recent addition. Those colors weren't natural. The gates were opened and closed by a man grabbing an enormous bar that extended from the gate, and leveraging the gate open by pushing his feet against stone steps like medieval ratchets. He maintained a useful tradition, though now one only used for recreation. The docks and marinas were collections of old and new pleasure craft: painted wood and poured plastic. I saw both go by. Both skippers looked happy.

The route was flat and quiet. The day was gorgeous. Low autumn sun drew longer shadows giving the land depth and contrast. The sweep of yellow rushes and deciduous leaves painted the prettiest day so far. Why couldn't the entire trip be endless repetitions of such a day? Maybe my mind was making progress. I was beginning to see what I wanted and enjoyed what I had.

After noon I was back on a long straight stretch of canal with a rumbly tummy. The views were marvelous, but there wasn't anywhere for food.

That's when I met the fishermen. Along a canal of nearly constant width, and I'm guessing nearly constant depth, a half-dozen men sat at nearly constant intervals. They fished about one cast away from each other. If they wanted more fish they should probably spread out, but the companionship was enough of a draw. They clustered by the coolers, all within earshot of each other's jokes and a short walk to the beverage box. We chatted. I continued. They had something, and someone, new to talk about. Maybe my story was the best catch of the day.

The canal heads to the sea, but not to a port. Somewhere I'd have to climb away from the canal and return to sidewalks and shoulders. I'd noticed a town called Denny, which immediately brought to mind big breakfasts at off-ramp diners in America. The image wasn't of the highest quality cuisine, but decades of branding messages reinforced a notion of reliability and an association with motels. Logically I knew not to count on advertisements from another continent, but my curiosity would take me there anyway. The canal flowed under a motorway. I couldn't read its signs, but a guess from the map, a cluster of houses on the opposite hill, and descending clouds convinced me to say good bye to the nicest trail of the trip and head north.

As soon as I turned away from the canal I found myself in a construction yard. That was a quick transition. Within a few steps the green, flat, quiet path became a rutted, messy, noisy enclave of diesels and heavy loads. Mud happens. I was alert and continually checking for traffic and signs. Opposing trucks stopped and blocked the road as the drivers visited through their open windows. I squeezed past along the pavement's edge. Something big was being built. The pavement was stressed and broken with no hint of a shoulder. They never saw me pass.

Thankfully, the road led to a relatively quiet neighborhood that apparently paralleled a highway. A road around the back side of the houses stayed farthest from the traffic noise and bordered the wetlands of a wide, flat valley. Some of the canal's peacefulness remained. My only concern was that I'd miss the main road and miss a place to stay. I couldn't get too lost as long as I was between the road and the canal. Besides, I was in suburbia. All I had to do was knock on enough doors until someone pointed me in the right direction. My map suggested that I was near the end of the Firth of Forth. I was near another opportunity to declare victory.

Side roads aren't known for excellent signage. The locals know where they're going and few tourists travel off the highway. Of course lost tourists would most appreciate directions. I wasn't lost, but I didn't know where I was. That's common. I knew that persistence would provide. My needs were the same whether I was sitting at home or on a walking tour in a foreign country: food and shelter. I was on a road. If I just kept walking I'd find what I needed.

The valley continued its march to the sea. The side road slowly angled up and out of the valley. My sweet views of grass fields edged in shrub trees were replaced with utilitarian views of houses, front yards, and light industry. The neighborhood looked large enough for restaurants and pubs, or at least fast food; but I realized that I hadn't seen many Open signs or people. Maybe I was walking through a bedroom community that emptied its residents to other towns or schools every day. Except for the details of the architecture, it felt like American suburbia. Even the machine shops had mostly empty parking lots.

One busy metal building, however, had a snack shack, a roach coach, a lunch wagon with enough room in it for one person, a small grill, and racks and bins for pre-packaged chips and junk food. It was the best looking eatery in view, because it was the only eatery in view. I was hunting for the town of Denny and thought that I'd found it. Asking for directions near Glasgow was such a fiasco that I decided to try buying some advice by buying something, anything, before I asked my questions. The only things she had to sell that my gluten-free diet would allow was a package of potato chips, also known as crisps. Evidently I wasn't in Denny, but I was headed the right way. I was approaching the town of Dennyloanhead, a name that sounded like one town name and two random words that bumped into each other on the printer's shelf and stuck together hard enough to make a very long city limit sign. She wished me well after delivering her concise advice. Maybe I would have learned more if I had bought more.

Across Scotland I never figured out the town name nomenclature. A dot on the map would have a name beside it, but variations on that name sprouted up around the town, probably modifying it to signify the north side, or the edge nearest the water, or the site of the ancient center, or whatever. I gave up trying to decipher them and settled on simply walking past enough signs until I found the one with the fewest letters.

Clouds crept in again. It was their familiar late afternoon taunt. Maybe it would rain or drizzle, but probably not. My stroll passed brick-walled front yards, some ancient, mostly current. The oldest were probably candidates for historical monuments except that there were so many of them that the road would be walled with bronze plaques as much as stacked stones. Each wall probably had enough stories for it's own geo version of a biography, which I guess would make it a geography, but of a different sort. A long line of historical markers would be silly, but it would have kept me entertained.

At least my way was paved, but I missed the canals. Roads are modern day canals. Will they be romantic some day? They're artifacts constructed to move people and things because the people and things aren't all in the same place. We move ourselves for working, schooling, and shopping that happen to be somewhere else. Traffic happens because economies of scale concentrate what we want and need. We have to go to it and them. We could get rid of a lot of traffic with a lot of home delivery, which only replaces many small cars with a few large and very busy trucks.

The street steered between opposing neighborhoods that had a lot in common. The houses were mostly about the same age, the same height, and the same shape. For the first few days I thought the houses had something cheap about them, even the old, storybook, solid ones. Subconsciously I was reacting to the short eaves. Most houses I've owned had eaves large enough to shade the windows, and to keep most of the rain away from the siding. Eaves in Scotland were stubs wide enough to attach a gutter and have room left for a downspout. Ivy has no problem negotiating the overhang. Swallows could barely find dry shelter in the narrow space. Homes with small eaves back home are most commonly mobiles, homes that save every penny in their construction and that won't extend a roof line because the house has to fit on a trailer that has to fit on the highway. Subconsciously, Scotland's houses struck me as a nation of mobile homes until I realized that stone and brick don't need protection from the rain, there may never be a day so hot that shade would be important, and because those houses were never going to move. Rooting out ingrained expectations takes time and reflection. It wasn't until I mentally probed around my attitude for days that I realized why my perception was skewed.

I guessed that I was approaching Denny because the housing aged. The stone walls were stouter. The roads weren't as straight. Pedestrians appeared again and assured me that there was lodging at the top of the hill. A fine old stone church, darkened with age deposited soot, and bordered by the largest patch of green looked like an anchor for the town. The intersection beyond was at the crown of the hill with streets spilling downhill away from the church, a betting parlor, a shop, and a pub. The church was outnumbered by vices two to one with one abstaining.

It was hard to tell the age of the pub because the building was framed in aluminum scaffolding and populated by a couple of workmen. I worried about finding the pub closed for renovation. Yea! The pub was still in business. Despite their great vantage point outside the second floor windows, the workers didn't know if the pub rented rooms. Maybe they just didn't like being asked a question while they were working. I stepped around the corner, under the scaffolding, and found two doors in one entryway. One was for drinks. The other was for rooms. I opened and walked through the one for rooms and found a door that led right back to the drinks. There were a lot of hinges in that small space.

The owner of the pub found a room for me. They also had drinks. They didn't have food, not even pub grub, but there were plenty of take-aways within a few blocks. I'd found a place to stay for the night and I'd walk to dinner.

My first impression was that this was the way to travel. They had more things available than any other hotel, inn, or B&B, and they were the cheapest. Line up a bunch of these and walking across Scotland would become easy and popular. Unfortunately, the price was explained by the broken television, the weak heat, the black-ish mold in the shower, the convoluted floor layout, and my basic desire to not touch anything. I'm not squeamish, but I discovered my limit. Just because they had something didn't mean it was worth using. Maybe I caught them between cleanings.

Food was going to be a walk, so after a shower where I shrunk from bumping into the stall's walls, I changed clothes and wandered a few blocks. There was a large library, a supermarket, plenty of shops, and take-aways. The rest of Denny was much more appealing than my room.

Libraries closed early in various towns so I took advantage of the fact that Denny's library was open. As usual, I had to tell a bit of my story to get a guest account, and then wait for a seat. Email, facebook, and stock sites were my main hits. Communicating with friends was partly for my benefit, partly for their curiosity. Checking my portfolio was a continual exercise in optimism, otherwise why would I be investing? I hoped that my portfolio would grow or even rocket while I was gone. Instead, the trip's credit card charges looked like they'd be with me for a while. Because I was checking in with friends and an online dating service, I waited a bit longer for a seat with some privacy. Being single and fifty was bad enough without the advice and commentary of fourteen year olds.

Afterwards, I bought some groceries for the next day and wandered back to the pub.

It was late afternoon, too early for dinner. The room was too dismal for a nap. I settled into the pub for drinks, a "normal" Guinness. At least I could count on the Guinness. A pint of my favorite creamy stout was my most reliable comfort zone.

As usual, I retreated to a seat in the corner, accompanied by my book, notepad, and pen. Was I hiding in my writing the way some hide behind a viewfinder, in front of a monitor, or between headphones? I cared a bit about the answer, but then relaxed and allowed myself to be on vacation. If I wanted to write, then write. At least I wasn't hiding in my house.

Dinner was take-away. Indian food is popular in the UK and I wanted to see if was different than the US version of Indian food. I envisioned something simple and that it would be delivered quickly, cheaply, and with a random attempt at quality. The shop was a small storefront with a high counter barricading the small customer area from the large, busy, noisy kitchen. The decor was spartan. The counter didn't even have a way to walk from the front to the back. It was unambiguously divisive. There were a few hard chairs and a long windowsill for seating. I placed my order from a confusing menu, stood there waiting for my dinner, then sat there, then got out my notepad and wrote there, then watched a few other people walk in who probably had called ahead. In the time I waited I went from being eager to eat early, then anxious as my blood sugar dropped. My reserves must have been on the edge when I walked in. Eventually I was handed a bag with lots of little boxes inside. I'd ordered kabob and expected something long and skinny, not cubic. When I got back to my dim room I found meats I couldn't identify, spicy deep-fried bread that smelled wonderful but that I'd have to avoid because of gluten, and some unidentifiable bits. Travel is an adventure and hunger convinced me to eat blindly what I guessed was safe. I shoveled it in. It was

Indian food with a Scottish accent, spicy, spartan and a bit hard to understand.

Be careful what you wish for, you may get it. The town had almost everything I wanted as a place to take a break or wait out a storm, but something wasn't quite right. Some parts were excellent. Books and food sustain me, so I was glad for the library and supermarket. Being able to blog was handy too. The town was big enough to wander around in, and I could probably spend a day walking its grid of streets getting a feel for how the place was laid out. But I knew that each expedition would take me back to a room that I wanted to avoid. I wanted out of the room as soon as possible.

I lay in bed, wearing my hat and jacket to stay warm, and wondered how such a trip would work back in the States. American rural is much too expansive. The gaps between towns are more likely to spread out over scores of miles instead of Scotland's typical dozen. Even following the highway up Whidbey Island, with one of the highest B&B concentrations in America, would require fifteen mile hikes without directions to the sweet places one or two miles down side roads. The Southwest is emptier and less pedestrian friendly. Maybe the Southeast could work along the coasts. The Northeast probably has the best layout if a walker could afford it. As for the middle of the country, the original Louisiana that stretched from the Gulf to the Missouri, even bicycling was a series of long days between stops.

I was glad I was in Scotland, even with Denny's quirks.

The pub's hotel operated as a truck stop for truckless workers. Late at night working men walked in after their shift. They bumped around in the kitchen, set the laundry to maximum, turned on the television in the lounge, popped some beers, and complained about work and each other. Drunken arguments were taken outside, which meant they ended up under my room's window. Welcome to reality. This was not sanitized traveling. I wasn't at a resort, just a refuge.

In the morning I'd have to wander around and find breakfast, and think about the route. There was a tangle of possibilities for crossing the firth. Should I cross a nearby bridge and wander the long way along a scenic shoreline route, or head inland towards larger towns and shorter routes? Dundee wasn't very far on the map. With a bit of smarts, persistence, and stamina I might make it to Aberdeen, days farther along the coast of the North Sea.

With luck I'd get some sleep without picking up a bug, or being eaten by one.

Stirling Rain

October 1
Denny - Blairlogie

    I woke early. My eyes were burning and my throat was complaining. Something unhealthy was happening, they weren't going to serve breakfast, so I had no reason to stay. I left quickly. Denny had almost everything I needed and wanted, but I'd hit the wrong spot at the wrong time.

    My morning route took me past the take-aways, the supermarket, and the library. Everything was convenient, and closed. That's when I met a regret. An extra block or two past the evening's walk took me to another pub with rooms to rent. The building was cleaner, the lights were brighter, it was closer to everything I visited the day before. If I'd walked one more block, if the locals had directed me just a bit farther, I might have taken my first rest day and had a different impression of Denny. I made the mistake of thinking there was only one choice. On too many other trips I have passed the first choice hoping for better and ended up adding miles to my day. If I'd been willing to explore, and been willing to backtrack, I might have found a town for a vacation within my vacation. It was my desire to not backtrack that kept me from finding such a sweet looking place. I doubted that they'd check me in before others had even woken up. I maintained my momentum.

Head down and straight ahead defined the morning. Stirling wasn't far, only a few miles, so I knew I'd get there before some people had breakfast. I'd decided to head to Stirling for the simple reason that it had the icon for visitors information beside it on the map. I was hungry but could take my time, wander into a large city, save enough energy to do some urban sightseeing, and relax. The city limit sign surprised me. It was unexpected, stouter than most, and anchored in dirt and foliage instead of concrete and asphalt. I'd passed through miles of intervening countryside without remembering farm or forest.

Stirling is historic, which is an interesting distinction in a country like Scotland. Castles, fortresses, battles, royalty, are concentrated in Stirling, or so I'd read. As a walking tourist I noticed a few extra signs, some older buildings, and a sense of time, but my route was through and to the northeast. I passed through neighborhoods and strolled by shops. Schools and apartments bordered my path. History was scattered about, not laid out in a line for my entertainment. The day was dark and not very inviting.

Cities confuse me. Route-finding in rural areas is easier because there are fewer choices. Country roads are pragmatic and only curve or bend to avoid an obstacle. City streets, especially roundabouts, seem designed to misdirect. City buildings hide landmarks. Horizons are concrete and artificial. Directions to a destination are arranged for optimum traffic flow, not simplicity or minimal distance. Somehow, and I don't know how, I ended up at the train station. Finally a landmark I could find on the map that was also connected to little hashed lines connecting to other dots.

Stirling sits at the last bit of the Firth of Forth, the eastern bay that touches the North Sea. I could have celebrated walking from coast-to-coast, but I couldn't see salt water. I could, however, redefine success, catch a train and ride back to Glasgow and home, but I didn't want to do that. As I denied that option I realized I wasn't walking across Scotland merely to create a cocktail party story. There was no feeling of success because I couldn't fool myself. I wasn't done. The good news was that every day's journey would be an incremental success. Stirling was a small first step that would eventually build. Bragging rights would accrue, but what was more apparent and important was that I would relax more. With each day a declared success, I could travel with less emphasis on goals and more emphasis on enjoyment. My return ticket was more than ten days away. There were miles to walk. I checked the train schedule and fees as a backup plan, bought some books at the station's store, and took advantage of the dry surroundings to put on my rain gear. The clouds were beginning to leak. It felt that the dawn had never fully arrived.

I had good timing. The rains started while I was in the station. By the time I walked a few blocks I was very glad for my rain gear. Without it I would have been dangerously soaked. I also knew that everything in my pack would be dry. After Kirkintilloch, everything in my pack was double wrapped in plastic. The wettest thing was me, from my sweat. I was prouder for my good timing and packing than for reaching Stirling. Personal goals can be inexplicable and more important than others' expectations.

At a confusing tangle of signs were two bridges. The close one was modern and for cars. The farther one was ancient stone and looked like it might be for pedestrians only. I couldn't be sure of either's destination. New bridges can accommodate cars well, but sometimes at the exclusion of pedestrians. Old bridges are impressive and can lead to beautiful dead ends. I almost made that mistake down in the Florida Keys. There's a reason why the road to Pigeon Key is quiet. Follow it and find that you have to backtrack a mile or two when you get to the end of the bridge.

The rain made everyone retreat into bubbles of plastic, either into raincoats or under umbrellas. Sightseeing involved looking up, which made me wet enough to skip that. As for directions or diversions, I wasn't going to stop mothers scurrying by with strollers who obviously were aimed at the nearest dry refuge. No one wanted to stand and talk in the downpour and I didn't want the babies to get wet either. For safety's sake, I headed to the old bridge and away from the cars on slick streets. Such a stout bridge must lead somewhere.

Simple choices place people in surprising places. I'd found Stirling Bridge, where the Scots beat the Brits hundreds of years ago. It is massive and looked like it is built to outlast the pyramids. Books and movies have probably been written about that bit of history. I'm a fan of history. I could've spent an hour or two there. But, I am also am not a fan of hypothermia. I only took enough time to read the plaque's title and continue along. The Scottish rain increased as if to drive me from the bridge as if I was British. I was just a wet Yankee.

The wind came up, so I kept my head down and my feet moving. Loitering wasn't a good idea and walking kept me warm.

My route luckily followed the tracks. With Stirling Bridge behind me and the tracks beside me I could be definite about where I was on the map, if I was brave enough to take it out in the rain. The tracks were across the street on my right. A string of houses were on my left. Every address seemed to also be a cheery B&B. That was encouraging. Maybe the rain was going to force me into a refuge within a walk of historic sites. Unfortunately, each B&B sign was accompanied with a "No Vacancy" sign. I wasn't quite ready to stop yet, but it was a long string of hope, disappointment, repeat. Evidently I'd arrived at the right place at the wrong time.

At the far end of town was an intersection, a break in the weather to get out my map, and make a choice. One choice climbed a hill crowned with some monument after which the road turned east. The other choice turned east first, headed towards a large town, but then wandered southeast to the coast. My goal was to the northeast. The shortest route for a car may be a long detour at highway speeds, but I was always walking near my speed limit. Straight lines made the quickest trip. I didn't look forward to that hill though.

I'd missed breakfast in Denny. My brain found that ironic. There'd been no grand slam in the morning. Instead, a late, cold morning found me in front of an Italian restaurant that touted its summer treats. Hunger, a chance to get dry, and an opportunity to ask for directions pulled me inside.

I apologized for my wet gear. It's Scotland. Wet happens. They were serving a late breakfast, and I ordered a cup of black tea against my doctor's suggestions.

The restaurant had two sections. I sat in the front, partly to not bump people with my wet clothes. There were a couple of counters for the ice cream or gelato. The decor was more Italian than Scottish, which was appropriate. The back was a bit darker, larger, and held more tables and more of the crowd. I tried to be innocuous, but whether sound carried well, or I spoke too loudly to the waiter, or the grapevine worked very efficiently, somehow half the people there became aware of what I was doing. The external Scottish stoicism was replaced with a community of support. They even offered rides, but that missed the point of my trip. My route options were analyzed amongst various tables. I answered questions from across the room as I ate. I listened to the possibilities. They were delivered with lots of enthusiasm and little useful information. No one knew of any other lodging within a few miles. They didn't need it. They were better with advice for an hour's drive away, but that was days away for me. The roads I considered quickly steered into rural land with little support. They all agreed though that I should visit the Wallace Monument, the tall tower I'd seen on the hill above the intersection. It was impressive, but I didn't want to climb a hill to climb a monument to look into clouds.

I also didn't want to guess wrong about who I thought Wallace was.

I heard a lot and learned little, so I stayed with my first choice which was to climb the hill. It was marked as steep, and they pointed out that it was slippery and dangerous and that I should take care climbing it. Just as I suspected, it was another heart-attack hill.

As I climbed I realized that I'd made progress since Cairnryan. I'd made progress within my body. I'd made progress within my psyche. The climb made me sweat. The conditions were far worse. The air was colder. Rain fell thick enough to send a stream of water down the road and over the curb. Cars splashed me but didn't change how wet I was. Despite the conditions, I felt better. The climb was uncomfortable enough that I was dismayed at the "No Vacancy" signs behind me. but I also knew that I felt much better than when I'd started, only several days earlier. Fear had diminished. My legs worked with more ease. I had greater confidence in my self and my body. I better understood my motivations and my goals. I knew that I was doing it because I wanted to be there. The dialogue with my internal coach carried me up the hill. I was still in the middle of the pep talk when I ran out of hill. It was raining. I was breathing heavy. I was sweaty and soaked, and I laughed at myself. I was braced for an arduous climb that would tax my stamina, but the hill was less than half as high as I'd thought. I cleared the external hurdle of the hill, and an internal hurdle that couldn't be named. My laugh was as meaningful as any cheer.

At the top of the hill was the National Wallace Monument, which is an impressive structure built to remember William Wallace, one of the victors of the battle at Stirling Bridge. My guess was right. I was able to confirm that much without going inside. Any enthusiasm for climbing the tower failed in the rain. I knew little about the history and, as with most monuments, the real setting for Wallace's life was probably not within the monument. I was probably walking across the land that he'd walked across, and I'd read about his story when I was warm and dry.

The daily search for lodging overwhelmed any sense of accomplishment, but I've learned to accept that. There's a line from the Tao Te Ching that goes something like, "The wise man never loses sight of the baggage cart." It may be a lost translation, because I can't find it in any copies of the book, but I love the pragmatism of the thought. Great insights can be worthless if the practical matters aren't tended. My soul made progress, but my body eventually needed a place to sleep, and that long line of "No Vacancy"s didn't settle a small anxiety. I carried enough for a bivouac, but a bivouac in a dismal downpour is a survival trial, not a quirky vacation night.

Above the clouds the sun should have been near its zenith. It was only about noon, but as my energy drained I tested myself against the onset of hypothermia. I've had incipient hypothermia on hikes and bikes. One way I could tell was it was encroaching was an unshakeable fatigue, difficulty in concentrating, and trouble walking in a straight line. I had tea for lunch, not a beer, and certainly not three; which is how I felt. There was no debate. As soon as I found a sign for lodging, I'd follow it.

After the monument the land turned rural, just like the folks in the restaurant had said it would. They didn't tell me that after the hill the land turned flat.

Evidently the only people that wanted to live away from the water were the farmers. Wide, flat, and open spaces can be scenic. They were canvases for clouds. Cattle calls were pastured fog horns. Colors were muted in the heavy noon-time dusk. The urban sidewalk deteriorated into a ragged shoulder with large puddles. The road narrowed and bent around fields and passed along forests. A trail system headed higher and away from the road. Some other day. I had the right boots, skills, and attitude, but not enough gear to wet camp comfortably.

The road straightened and disappeared into a misted horizon, a view that showed no sign of changing. According to the local guides, hours of walking wouldn't change that. One cluster of homes raised my hopes, but it was even too small for a pub. As I watched my hope fade though, a B&B sign pointed down a farm lane. The lane looked empty, with no buildings in sight, but there was a grove of trees about a quarter mile away. There was no shoulder. Even the road was puddled. There was traffic in and out, which was encouraging, but also a hazard because their visibility was poor and the lane was narrow. I danced along the grass beside the road and finally arrived at a farmhouse that had turned itself into a B&B, restaurant, and gift shop. Very trendy. I was very wet, and happy for any roof in a storm. What I found was a functional estate.

The B&B was in the original farmhouse. I knocked and the farmwife welcomed me in, and agreed that dropping most of my foul weather gear in the covered alcove would be a very good idea. Her mini-hothouse plants were misted with the fragrance of wet boots and sweaty jacket. I sniffled as I followed her to my room.

It was a true farmhouse, not something built to tap into the tourist trade, even though that was its new role. The walls were thick enough to block any noisy evidence of the storm outside. The doorways were short enough that, after the first bump, I ducked at every door. The beds were tiny. I had the boys' room. The farmwife, now also hostess, had turned her family house into lodging. The furnishings may have changed, but the house was authentic to the point that I had to curl my body onto a bed made for a teenager. The two narrow beds seemed more appropriate to a sixties sit-com instead of a romantic B&B, but maybe romance was different in Scotland. At least the room was big, so I was able to spread everything out to dry. The plastic bags worked, almost.

My nap was long because it was much more comfortable than my night in Denny. I almost slept through the end of lunch. By the time I got to the restaurant they were closing for the day and out of almost everything except some soup. Closing for the day was a major inconvenience. Where would I get dinner? They assured me that it was a quick ride back into Stirling. I told them that I didn't have a car. They told me about the gift shop. I imagined candy bars and beef jerky, so I ate everything they brought with the lunch. Garnishes have at least some calories.

The gift shop was a joy and a surprise. It wonderfully went beyond snacks and trinkets. It was as large as a small grocery, and filled with high-end food. Much of it was meant to be cooked: culinary explorations to play with in a full kitchen. I didn't have that option but I filled my basket with foods that didn't need refrigeration. What started as a hardship turned into a classic plate: smoked salmon, cheese, crackers, wine, macaroons, and nibble food for the evening and the next day's walk. The presentation was less than stellar, but the setting was warm and appreciated.

The clerks commented on my choices and I told them about my walk. They were walkers too, and thought that walking back to town wouldn't be too far. True, but not for me and my start in Denny. He had just walked the West Highland Way, which is some ninety miles long. She had just walked fifteen miles in a day, beating my average. We compared notes. They showed me photos and their map, which they'd turned into a display in the shop. They were very familiar with the farmhouse. He was one of the sons who'd grown up and moved out. I was sleeping in his room and probably his childhood bed. He wouldn't fit in it either.

My evening was long and quiet. The thick farmhouse walls blocked out the noise of the storm and the livestock. My entertainment was quietly provided by the books I bought in Stirling. The only noise to listen for was the sound of the bathroom latch. It was a shared facility, and a bit of listening saved some knocking. Otherwise the other lodgers didn't make a sound.

The only things that interrupted my sleep were my sniffles. I was glad I stopped early.

Manifest A Destination

October 2
Blairlogie - Fossoway

Bumps in the morning and throughout the night were the guests maneuvering their way around beds and in and out of the bathroom. Despite the noises the breakfast room was nearly empty when I sat down for the usual Scottish scrambled eggs, ham-ish bacon, and toast. I saw one guest. We chatted for a short while. He didn't seem to be interested in anything outside his world. He ate and then he was gone. Breakfast wasn't entertaining, but it was real.

The weather cleared in the night. Freshly fed and ready for a longer day, I walked outside and found impressive stone hills less than a mile away. I'd walked beside them while they were hidden by fog. Those forest trails probably led to impressive panoramas. I miss climbing mountains. One of my dependable joys is reaching a summit and seeing a panorama. If there was a mountain route straight to Aberdeen I would've been tempted. Every day would probably deliver a stupendous view or two, but the coastal route and its promise of comfort was more appealing. I enjoy it all, climbing mountains, hiking ridges, and walking beaches. Scotland has it all. Scotland also has pubs and pubs are placed beside pavement, so back to the road I went.

Leaves were beginning to turn. The heather on the hill was already russet. Fog framed the hill be cropping the ridge making it easier to concentrate on the foliage.

As the sun burned off the fog I was gradually treated to blue sky. It was almost t-shirt weather, but three days of hiking in the rain convinced me to re-warm my core by wearing an extra layer. Sunshine was welcome, but started by warming my skin. My exertions started in my core and worked their way out. The two sources worked well together. When I began to sweat it was time to shed the shell.

Routefinding was simple. Go east. Go straight. The road had no desire to challenge the hill and the hill pointed to the sea.

I showed up in Alva so early that the shops weren't open. The architecture was familiar: old stone walls, square brick houses with no eaves, chimneys sprouting spouts without smoke. Yet, the town was more inviting than most. The sidewalks were broader.

The road was wider. More light came into the space. There was probably enough room for trees to line the streets, and maybe they did at one time, but parked cars were more prevalent.

Maybe it would have been worth the push through yesterday's afternoon, but choices had to be made, and hypothermia isn't a pleasant playground. The matter was moot, so I didn't second guess myself. I just kept walking.

Second guessing is too common throughout life. I avoided the performance anxiety produced by an imposed itinerary, but a persistent logistical remained. How far could I walk and where should I stop for the night? Both were sources of mental effort. In either case, the past didn't matter. I was always in a new here and tasked with deciding which there to use as a goal. I was on a sidewalk heading east. For miles my choice would only be to place the next step one stride away in the same direction. Choices only happened at intersections and they were far apart. The fewer choices I had, the easier it was to relax and enjoy. At a walker's pace the scenery went slowly by.

Sunshine prevailed and the nice part of autumn wrapped around me.

Usually the pedestrian pavement vanished within a hundred yards of the town limits. Randomly, sidewalks would show up, as if a road crew had a bit extra concrete, or were given orders to pave the wrong place. While dancing in and out of traffic along the pocked, grassy shoulder I'd come across a bit of relief. Sometimes I'd notice a sidewalk on the other side of the road. Looking over my shoulder I'd see that it had been there for a while, but I'd missed it because I was so intent on not twisting an ankle, and not getting hit by traffic. Worries at my feet kept me from seeing a better way. The only way to notice the better way was to stop and look away from my worries. It was much appreciated when the better way simply showed up in front of me.

Farms stretched away across flatlands to my right. To my left, the farmlands gently sloped, transitioned to inclined forest, and then became steep, rocky hillside. I walked the border between two lands, two geographies, one that accommodated us and our agriculture, the other that naturally maintained its dominance through simple defiant existence.

I found the town of Dollar. Nice town. It was greener and cleaner but maybe the sunshine gets the credit. As I walked through town it was noticeably more alive. It was late morning. People ran chores. Shops were open. It was far too early to get a room, and the weather was cooperating, which I wanted to enjoy on foot. But Dollar was so appealing that I stopped in at a hotel that seemed to have everything I needed. It looked like a nice backup plan, especially walking into increasingly rural areas that folks told me were devoid of services. The hotel and the staff were nice, and even pointed out that the town of Muckhart probably had lodging too. They knew more about their neighborhood than most.

People's horizons continually surprise me. Very few people know what's ten miles down the road. Most horizons are defined by the range required by their chores. Few step beyond those limits, or are aware of what is one road over from their habitual route. There's an ecological benefit to communities that sustain themselves, but there's a social loss if there is little reason to extend community to the next community. I rarely found worthwhile advice about lodging, even from other inn-keepers. Our worlds can become very small, and if our small world is very comfortable it can be easy to never look outside it. I was glad that I got myself out of my house and into and across another country.

My cheery visit to Dollar was short. Blue skies don't last forever. Soon after I left it, and soon after noon the clouds returned. They too would eventually step aside for more than a few hours, wouldn't they?

I'd been cautioned about the road ahead. I was walking into sparse lands. Motorways carried away most of the traffic. Tourists skipped the direct but slow rural routes. The motorways were quicker. The more scenic route was a few extra driving minutes away along the shore with views and golf courses. My path was straighter and lonelier. I probably wasn't allowed on the motorway, and a diversion of a few minutes drive would add days of walking. At least traveling on lonely rural roads is quiet. Unfortunately, traveling on tired legs is a bit daunting when there is no support in sight.

Rosehips kept me company. The flowers were gone and left red berries along the walls and fences. In full bloom the walk would have been accompanied by petals and bees. It would've taken longer too, if I was there in the right season with the right camera.

Muckhart straddled the road. There were signs to B&Bs, but no distances were marked. A turn to a B&B could be a ten mile detour, or a walk around a corner. I followed the main road in search of a pub, without expecting more. The town wasn't tall enough for a hotel and I hadn't found a motel in Scotland.

It was after another missed lunch when I found a classic, long low public house fringed with cars. In a rare event, one of the patrons asked if I needed directions. A Scot starting a conversation with me was a surprise. I asked him about B&Bs. He didn't know of any but thought the barkeep would have some good advice. Evidently barkeeps are unofficial information sources. I don't like asking for advice from someone when they are busy, but I accepted the invitation. Pack on my back I walked in and found a friendly and active fellow busy behind the bar. He knew of a place or two in the neighborhood but thought they were all booked. I should try backtracking a half mile to one of them, and if that didn't work, there might be one on the top of the town. I didn't want to take anymore of his time. He was in the rush of a full house, time was money, and I wasn't spending any until I had a room.

I rarely backtrack. Progress is going forward. Every step is a ratchet towards a goal. Besides, empty rooms behind me can be filled in the time it takes me to walk back to them.

A sign angled back past painted walls around a curve and down a lane. Distances are notoriously wrong when people give directions because they are thinking in car terms, not strides. I didn't want the rooms to be "just a couple more miles.", but after my experience at Denny I was willing to explore a little. Down the lane, down the slope, and hunt for a sign that eventually pointed to a suburban brick rambler. It wasn't historic or quaint, but if they had a room it would be great. A knock on the door produced nothing. Standing there, not wanting to rush anyone, I watched the weather thicken. The sky was darker and the wind picked up. I knocked again. Footsteps were followed by a young matron with babe on hip. She didn't want to answer because of the baby and the dogs, and it wasn't her establishment. She was just watching things for the owners. There was no room. I thanked her and quietly turned away disappointed.

One road leads to another, and there was a trail sign beside the house that suggested a shortcut back to the road. It also pointed out to a field. I didn't want to wander yet another pasture at the end of the day as rain came in.

I backtracked my backtracking and continued along the road looking for the top of the town and the rumored rooms.

The houses thinned. The stone walls ended. The sidewalk turned to grass. But the land had buildings amongst the fields and pastures. Maybe one of them was a B&B. Optimism was necessary, but it wasn't based on much more than one phrase caught in a pub and a bit of hope.

Muckhart looked small but it's variations spread far along the road. In addition to Muckhart there is the Pool of Muckhart and Yetts of Muckhart. I wondered why anyone would name anything Muckhart unless it was in a Tolkien-ish fantasy novel. It probably made more sense in ancient Scottish. Maybe Pool and Yetts expected to become the suburbs of a metropolis called Muckhart. The farms were proof that hadn't happened. I shrugged and thanked an interesting town name for some mindless mental distraction. The less I thought about tired legs the easier it was to keep walking.

Sprinkles began. I expected them. Again I wondered why I was walking in Scotland in the autumn, but I had that answer ready. I wanted to walk Scotland, and I could do it in the autumn. The logic was somewhat circular and wasn't required to be any more robust than that. The t-shirt weather had been gone for hours. My rain gear came out of the pack, and so did the map. I found myself at an intersection. My strategy was to head to Dundee, but pragmatically it might make more sense to head north and find a room. Realistic logistics alter grand plans. As I tried to divine the possibility of clusters of civilization from slight squiggles on my map of Scotland, the rain moistened the paper. With golf courses and race tracks in the vicinity it seemed that there would be lots of choices, but there were no signs or marks. My main choice was to continue and hope. It was a long day and getting longer.

I was concerned. It was October. The sun and the horizon met sooner every day. The weather was consistently turning towards winter. It was a Saturday which probably explained the lack of buses. It might be a long wait at the bus stop. Even if I caught a ride without having to wait overnight, it would mean rewalking from Dollar through Muckhart and into the unknown again. My legs were tired and my enthusiasm was reduced to thin hope.

The wind turned and the sprinkles became determined rain.

An intersection arrived. Staring at the two choices wasn't going to produce a magic glowing arrow. To the left was uphill and north. A bit to the right was the valley and farmland. I tried staring anyway, but squinting didn't produce a sign. If three cars had taken one or the other turn I probably would've followed them. No one came by. I turned to the right and followed the valley. Either choice would have been based on hope. Turning right simply meant not having to head north and uphill as heavy weather approached.

After the intersection the road dipped and curved and I wondered if the rest of the day would be snippets of views shrunken by weather, with a series of raised then deflated expectations. I had too many days of re-inflating popped bubbles. One of my best tools is perseverance. It pedaled me across America. At that point all I knew was that perseverance might have to carry me to a bivouac at dusk.

I joked with myself about Scottish mirages. Instead of palm trees around oases a Scottish mirage might be a "Guinness Is Good For You!" sign in a pub window. I also chided myself for silly optimism that might get me into trouble.

Within a mile of my most dismal introspections was a small oval sign across from a drive. I'd like to say I manifested the part that said, "B&B." At first I thought it was just another house sign posted so friends could find an isolated driveway along an empty road. As I got closer I chuckled because I hadn't expected to see B&B, and because it didn't say much more than that. Just an arrow pointing to a climbing drive. I knew that I'd take anything I could get, one star or five stars. It didn't matter as long as they had a room. I restrained my hope in case I found a "No Vacancy" sign, or a board stating "Closed for the Season." Stirling's season was over and it was only a short drive away. It looked like the trend continued. The driveway and parking area were empty. The place was quiet. It was also new, modern, well-landscaped, and looked like someone's custom-designed dream home. There was even a porch where I could get some temporary shelter. I clomped my way up to the front door and knocked. And waited. And wondered if anyone was home.

About the time I was considering taking a seat and a nap, a woman came to the door and politely and uncertainly greeted me. I was a surprise. She hadn't expected guests and she hadn't heard a car pull up. It was after the main season. They had only opened a few months earlier and hadn't advertised much. How did I ever find them? I possibly put her in the entrepreneur's dilemma. If someone showed up they'd make some money. If no one showed up they could get a rare day off from work. In a short while she welcomed me in, pleased to have a guest, especially one that left the wettest and muddiest gear outside. She gave me a tour of the house, gave me one of the best rooms, and gave me their story.

They lived there for years and ran the land as a nursery. That explained the fine landscaping; but, nursery work was harder than their bodies appreciated. Rather than continuing to do something that eventually may hurt them, they decided to change while they could instead of after they had to. They closed the nursery, rebuilt the house, and re-opened as a bed and breakfast. Evidently they didn't want to be like every other old B&B because the rooms, the furniture, the decor, the plumbing, were all modern while remaining Scottish. It was a welcome change. Balancing progress and tradition can be difficult. I liked their style.

There was still plenty of time before dinner so I went up to my room, luxuriated in a wonderful shower where the hot water worked, learned how deeply the cold had soaked into my core despite my efforts, and snuggled myself under the covers for a warming nap. The rain drummed on the skylight. Power naps are amazing rejuvenators. Within an hour I was up and wandering around the house. How much farther could I go each day if I could find places to nap beside the road without looking homeless? Could a short rest double my progress?

Her partner wandered through on his way to work on a gate in the mist and rain. I offered to help. It is fun surprising people. He looked at me as if he'd never had a stranger offer a hand before, especially a tired stranger who was staying with them to rest and get out of the rain. He was wise enough to not turn down free help. Luckily, the gate was under an awning. We spent about an hour fussing with the normal house repair frustrations: tools in the wrong place, missing pieces, knots in wood where holes need to be drilled, structures that aren't as straight as they could or should be. He wondered why I was walking across Scotland and why I was willing to help instead of rest. I helped because I wanted to help. It wasn't out of obligation. I was paying them for the room. It got back to the very reason I wasn't drunk on a beach. The best way for me to relax is to live, but at my own pace doing things of my own choosing. He was in the midst of another of an never-ending set of chores. I was merely holding up the gate and enjoying a quiet and pleasant conversation. That hour was more memorable than miles of walking.

An insight into Scottish wisdom was delivered by a can of varnish, "If you do what it says on the tin, the product will do what it says on the tin." Why do we make things more complicated than that?

There wasn't any place for dinner within walking distance so they let me join them. It was the first enjoyable meal-time conversation I'd had in Scotland. I felt that intruding on the rest of their evening wasn't included in the price so I retreated to read and rest in my room. A few minutes later he knocked on my door. A couple of my sniffles and coughs at dinner convinced him to pass along some advice. A dram or two will help cure my ills. He invited me down to sit by the fireplace and sip some whisky.

For the next two hours we chatted and sipped. We shared stories about land management. Land use planning was part of his job. I was site steward for a land trust. He has to consider Roman ruins. I only have to tackle invasive plants like English Ivy and Scotch Broom. I pointed out that some English and Scottish plants aren't welcome in America. I should've asked him if there were any other invasive Americans in Scotland.

He was right. Time by the fire with a dram at hand healed many aches.

Crash And Indulgence

October 3
Fossoway - Glenfarg

     Whisky before bedtime has other benefits besides curing a sore throat. My dreams were memorable and insightful. Episodes from childhood were replayed with a twist that revealed the foundations of familiar stresses. My habits reached back decades instead of just years. Today's effect from yesterday's cause was also from last year's cause, last decade's cause, but really from those first few years when my attitudes about life were learned. Do what you should and it will all be good, except that I hadn't learned that doing what I wanted was one of the shoulds.

Each day my stress reduced by layers. I'd see a source, and if I worked through it, some group of muscles would relax. I'd enjoy that for a while, and then I'd notice another tightness. My stress didn't dial down smoothly. It dropped in steps with occasional stumbles. Some stresses laughed at me when I discovered them, as if they were playing a game of hide and seek. It wouldn't all vanish in a moment, a day, or even a vacation. My attitude and perspective was changing as I recognized each source and consequence. Stress relief was one of the reasons for the trip. Evidently my time spent sleeping was as important as my time spent walking.

Sprinkles dotted the skylight. I packed slowly, waiting for a change in the weather, or at least a shift to a tailwind. It didn't matter. The rain had its own schedule.

The countryside was more rural than any other place except that sheep pasture. There was no attempt at sidewalks or shoulders. I walked the asphalt and dodged rare traffic by standing still in the rough, wet grass. Farmhouses were less than a car's width from the pavement. Someone's plan for a farm and someone's plan for a road almost collided. As long as the farmers slept on the far side of the house they might get a quiet night's sleep.

I found sidewalks in the town of Milnathort, but I arrived before the inns were open. The grocery was the only busy business.

The land passed quickly because I didn't stop to take photos. So much for the image of me as a professional photographer. I only carried a point and shoot, and I was on vacation. The full-size digital SLR would have reminded me of depths of field, tripods, and constantly cleaning my lenses. My camera fit in a pocket and had an automatic lens cover. It couldn't do as much, but it weighed a lot less, and gave me a lot less to worry about. It also meant that I missed a lot of great photos, but I didn't want to walk across Scotland hiding behind a viewfinder. Why put another layer between me and my experience? My mind remembered many of the missed images, and selective amnesia does a wonderful job of editing. Maybe with the right lens, and a tripod, and a lot of lens cleaning I might have grabbed Pulitzer images; but it was more likely that I'd just end up walking slower, not getting as far, and trying to keep the batteries charged.

My writer friends probably had a similar lament. Even my notes were brief. I wrote enough to entertain myself and to nudge my memory. No transcripts were necessary. Anything that built towards a book was secondary. I didn't feel the need to emulate Cahill or Krakauer.

Sights that are never seen on tours slowly arrived and passed by. Old WWII airfields were turned over to modern ultra-lights. I guessed at the age, but thought the particular bald eagle emblem looked like it belonged to the US Army Air Corps. Old, possibly historic farmhouses were quaint and dwarfed by the metal buildings operating from the economy of scale. Old stone defined the place, but new metal was five times the size, used more often, and hard to ignore.

Beyond Milnathort was a choice, again. At an innocuous intersection surrounded by open land I had to choose between east and somehow eventually crossing the Firth of Tay, or north and aiming for a land route through Perth. The Firth of Tay wasn't tiny and on the map its near shore looked like a road without enough dots. It seemed devoid of lodging. North wasn't much better. The map showed only a motorway heading to Perth, but the real world showed me an intersection with a pedestrian-friendly rural road and a jewel of a sign. Glenfarg Hotel this way. That sounded good enough for me. I had to thank them for their sign. Without it my route selection would have been no better than a coin flip.

My itinerary tensions eased. My route choices were narrowing. After Perth, I'd be walking with saltwater on my right. The coast of the North Sea was stitched with towns that had little tourist i's dotting the map. I'd easily make it to Dundee, and might make it to Aberdeen.

The only people I saw passed me on horses. The land was tamed into pastures and fields. Some of the houses were mini-farms immaculately tended. Either the owners were continually painting and fixing, possibly forgetting their crops; or they were spending a lot of money on a rural maid service. Long views under the cloud deck stretched to green plains. The weather made the air feel like the North Sea was reaching inland to claim territory. Feathered hoofed draft horses shared a pasture with shaggy ponies. Neither looked affected by the weather.

Miles scrolled by without evidence of a town. I knew I hadn't imagined the sign, but doubt showed up anyway. An internal emotional support failed and my confidence crashed as hard as it had after the 18 miles into Glasgow. I watched it happen and fought it. Why would it happen? I'd finally eaten well, stayed with companionable folk, and had put miles and days between me and that room above the pub door in Denny. My goal was near. I'd learned that every moment held every emotion, and that all I had to do was choose. I chose joy but couldn't find it. My tension rose and body aches amplified. It was frustrating to watch it happen and not be able to will the episode away. Maybe finally realizing that I'd reach the coast released an anxiety that I wouldn't make it. Maybe my mind relaxed too quickly and my body found itself no longer struggling against an opposing force. I threw theories around but nothing made a difference. My pains became a chorus and declared it was time to stop.

Glenfarg hid beyond the horizon by hiding in a vale. Finding the town gave me some small relief, or it might have been that walking downhill was welcomed by my tired legs. Buildings went by and I tried to imagine the hotel from a few words on a sign. The hotel made it easy on me. It wasn't hiding. It was the largest building in town, designed to look like a four story castle, which, considering Scotland, maybe it was at one time. It looked expensive and it looked like it had no competition. I'd pay their price. Expensive was less important than finding a place to rest a suddenly exhausted body, mind, and spirit.

The main thing I remember about my room was that as soon as I was done with my nap, the sun came through and blue sky followed it.

Mood affects mood. Rather than be caught in a downward spiral, I fed and watered myself, hoping that it was fuel or fluids that I needed. I snuck in a late lunch before the kitchen shut down for its afternoon break. Potato soup and Guinness.

The staff worked like a quiet crowd of concierges, completing tasks without fuss, and jumping to them on the mildest of suggestions, which threw me into a verbal filter. These are the sort of folks that would start up a band if I wanted some music. I didn't want that much fuss. But then, I'm the sort of traveler that would prefer to be given free run of the kitchen rather than be attended by a uniformed waiter.

Wandering around town was a short, understated event, just long enough to prove to myself that my collapse was temporary. Episodes might continue to happen, but the recovery times were down to minutes instead of days.

The buildings were stout. A visit in a few decades wouldn't change a slate roof, or the massive stone blocks that framed windows. It looked like the town can't grow or sprawl. Geography bounds and preserves it. Hills surround it, and the ground slopes and drains it. I wondered what feng shui would say about that. Travelers from a century ago would probably recognize the place, and would have to search for a newspaper to find the date.

I ate and relaxed by reading and writing. My notebook was an excellent listener. I let my thoughts flow and realized that my conscious mind couldn't pin labels on the progress and revelations being discovered by my subconscious. Unknowable things percolated in my back brain. As I sat down to dinner, with a notebook and a table for one, a wave of awakening rose from the top of my spine through the back of my head. A mild swell of wellness swept through me. I welcomed it, but was it revelation, time, cheese, or Guinness? The cause wasn't as important as the effect. My vacation was worth the effort and the price. Stress was reducing in a way that couldn't be included on an itinerary.

Various people considered joining me on the trip, but we probably would have taken different routes, found different stops, taken different detours.

The companionship would have been appreciated, but maybe my mind needed the time alone. Maybe that mood crash showed up because something was determined to make me stop and stay at Glenfarg. It drained my energy to serve its agenda.

A massive plate of roast beef arrived. There was a good chance that I hadn't eaten much red meat lately. Maybe that was the simple explanation. I turned and tipped the plate to drain off sauce that threatened to drown the potatoes. The greens were eaten first. Leafy greens were so rare that I treated them like a delicacy. Smashed peas stood in for vegetables. Scottish cuisine is usually meat, potato, and vegetable, but without the vegetable. I ate 50% more than usual, possibly more. I didn't guess at calories. I was due for a feast. Whether it was calories, vitamins, minerals, or comfort somewhere in a big pile of food would be enough stuff to recharge my batteries.

I received impeccable service because I stopped at a well-respected, well-known destination hotel. They were there for a fancier clientele. Some stylish gentlemen from "south" strolled in for the next day's hunt. They had a drink before checking in, so that after they checked in, there'd be enough time for a drink before dinner. How about drinks between each course? I wondered. I also wondered how they early they'd start drinking and hunting the next morning. I hoped I was headed in a different direction.

My thoughts flowed into my notebook. More pages were used than any other night. I noticed that the flow was restricted by language and how fast I could write. Thoughts slipped by and evaporated while waiting their turn to meet the page. I could type faster than write, but was glad that I hadn't brought a computer. What ended up in the notebook probably wasn't as important as the time I spent paying attention to my thoughts and emotions.

Up in the room I continued to write, partly to capture thoughts that circled back but mostly because the television only showed two channels, a reality show travesty and music videos. The magazines were in a foreign language and about architecture and interior design. The pictures were pretty, but couldn't hold my attention. I was going through withdrawals from my book-a-day habit.

I ended the day, fueled, rested and packing clean clothes. During the afternoon the staff went out of their way to run a change of clothes through their laundry. I smelled better. I wondered if they'd do the same for the hunters, assuming they come back safe.

Down And Up And Down And Out

October 4
Glenfarg - Glencarse

Dreams were appreciated but the images faded fast. The feelings remained. Breakthroughs and insights were delivered cryptically, but I felt like I was making internal progress. Deciphering the details could be my mental entertainment for the day's walk.

I was up early and eager to go; but, despite the hunters, the restaurant was not. Breakfast wasn't served until 8:30. I was usually walking by then. It seemed that the more I spent for the room the later breakfast was served. They were nice enough to accommodate me with very buttery scrambled eggs, salty smoked salmon, and sugary orange juice. I fueled myself as a defense against repeating the previous day's deficit.

As I checked out, one of the staff shyly asked, "Aren't you lonely doing this?" Never in my eleven weeks of bicycling across America did anyone ask me that. Then the most common comment was, "Oh, I could never do that.", which always struck me as defeatist and evidence of a faded America. A proud American, back in some stereotypical era that maybe never existed, would have said, "I don't want to do that."; not that they can't, but that they don't want to. It was assumed that anyone could do anything they committed themselves to, they just might not want to spend eleven weeks on a bike seat. In Scotland, the comment was empathic, an interest in how I felt during my adventure. The short version of my answer was, "Mostly, no." From their expression I suspect that they expected, "Mostly, yes."

The weather was dry and encouraging. It looked like the prelude to a warm, dry, sunny day; a good day for a walk.

I'd walked down a vale to get into Glenfarg, and the slope continued. My route passed into deeper and contorted territory. Town passed behind me soon and the road entered a narrowing valley reminiscent of West Virginia: no shoulder, steep valley walls shielding the floor from sunlight, high humidity like a fog or dew that knew it didn't have to dissipate, and heavy rumbling truck traffic, though it wasn't coal trucks but haulers headed to the landfill. There was rarely a straight section as the road negotiated a meandering line between the hillsides and the stream. The curves were tight enough that the trucks leaned into each apex and forced me to jump into the bushes. At least the traffic constantly trimmed the hedges, so it was easy to guess how far I had to jump. My quiet, sunny stroll was replaced with a tentative trek through shadows.

I took a break beneath a tall, arched, stone and concrete bridge that crossed the valley. The blocks were regular, so I guessed that it was more modern, but the moss and ferns took advantage of the dampness to establish colonies aging the structure. With a bit more effort the foliage would hide the stonework. It was a great setting for a medieval novel. The longer I sat the easier it was to imagine ancient races, ruins, bizarre creatures, and things hiding just out of sight. Fantasizing was fine, but the dismal light steered my mood towards gloom. I wanted a lighter mood so a short break was best.

Cars pass through such terrain within minutes. It took me longer. Before pavement it may have taken hours. There were a few signs of buildings that looked like they predated asphalt. Maybe they were from a time when travel was slower and people were more likely to stop at dusk rather than push on into the dark. They persisted out of habit.

The road drained into flatlands and left the valley behind. My world had gone from cramped and sullen to expansive and uplifting. The sun was there all along, but the geography and foliage along the deep rut of my morning route obscured it. Maybe I was walking onto another river's floodplain or ancient tidelands. Openness and the sunshine were only rumors back in the shady valley. As I walked and warmed, my posture and mood improved. A bicyclist came by, packed for the long haul. He didn't stop, but shouted out that he was headed to Cape Town, South Africa. There is always someone going farther and with a completely different style. He was headed up and into the canyon I'd just left. I shuddered at the thought. Bicycles, especially ones loaded to cross continents, can't easily jump into bushes. He had enthusiasm on his side.

Open land at the edge of rugged terrain meant an opportunity for roads to cross, intersect, and confuse my sense of direction. I was headed to Perth. Like Stirling, Perth sat at the head of a firth, an inland safe route that avoided long hops across water. Roads swept into curves to help cars accelerate and decelerate; but roundabouts don't readily announce their ultimate direction. Simple perpendicular intersections are appreciated. My trip was plans made from guesses, and I guessed that going straight would keep me on smaller roads, off any motorway, and hopefully would steer me through a town.

I entered a town small enough to be cute but too small for a stop and a stay. But cuteness was appreciated. Even a precinct house was adorned with a mural, which was a significant contrast to the blockhouse outside Glasgow. The land lay flat only as it crossed the floodplain, but soon enough the road curved and climbed as it reached more solid ground. Stones were plentiful enough to be stacked into head-high farm walls that restricted my view. Traffic acoustics were channeled back with reverb. If the walls were shorter I would have been able to see the farm at work, but sight isn't the only sense. Evidently, it was time to spread the manure.

For all I knew I was heading into the highlands. Scotland is famed for its highlands and the land was tipped up. Fortunately, I was climbing with less effort and no heart attack worries. About the time I thought I might have missed a turn and was headed around Perth instead of through it, I met dog walkers. Dog walkers are to a city what seagulls are to the shore, signs that homes are near. The dog walkers gave better directions. I crossed over a high point and looked down onto Perth with a view that so good that I was surprised it wasn't snagged by a high-end restaurant. A green ridge to the right, bordered by a winding river bottom, flowed past a waterside city. The world was lush and bright, and Perth looked inviting.

Downhill was such a relief. Walking into a bright city was nice too. It wasn't Dundee on the sea, but Perth had a feeling of personal destination that I hadn't expected. Maybe it was the size of the city. There was architecture. There were parks. There was sidewalk take-away for lunch, the first in days. There were also incomprehensible directions. One fine miss heard where I was trying to go, pointed me ahead, motioned that I should keep going a mile or so, then turn right at that last landmark, you know, the one past the one-inch. She was so enthusiastic that I thanked her and walked along before realizing I had no idea what she meant by the one-inch. About halfway along a soccer field I realized that the grass was about one inch tall. I turned right.

Or I was about to when I noticed that a sign pointing to the left for a tourist information center; but signs pointing to i without distances could be multi-mile detours, or just down the block. I gave it a try. I walked two blocks, couldn't find another sign, gave up, pivoted around, and returned to the path she'd suggested.

Perth was worth exploring. Glasgow was built as impressively, but was too close for my taste. Besides, it always rained there. The streets and buildings I'd seen in Glasgow crowded each other and pulled in sightlines and boundaries. Perth had more air, and sunlight. The buildings were as solidly built, but the stone and concrete was lighter. They were also farther apart. If I arrived later, I may have stayed. But it was a walker's day and I wanted to make it to Aberdeen. The only way to reach my goal was to not stop. I just kept walking. My path took angular turns completely unlike suburban onramps. Shoulders, sidewalks and beaten paths were replaced with broad, stone, scenic walkways along the water and public venues. There were definite advantages to walking in the right city.

Across the bridge, which I'd seen miles ago from atop the hill, I stepped past a riverside park, well-tended and populated. Its paths were appealing, but I didn't know where they led. Instead, I paralleled them while walking along the main road through established neighborhoods of brick homes and tended gardens, ever on the lookout for clues about what came next. Between Perth and Dundee was about twenty miles of dot-less motorway according to my map. I wasn't allowed to walk on motorways, and even if I could, I didn't know if there'd be places to stay. Perth could be a pedestrian dead-end, pleasant, but disappointing if that was the case.

One last park outside of town had doughnut-turfed landscaping. A car of young folk added to it by driving over the curb onto the grass below the Perth city limits sign, taking their group photo, and continuing on their hormonal trek. Hey, kids, get off the lawn!

After them the world quieted down except for easily ignored highway noise.

The world quieted down as the city fell away. The sidewalk faded too. Broad concrete turned to shoulder turned to dirt footpath. I walked towards the water and greener, more open land. The pavement curled away into a highway interchange with a span of concrete overhead. I doubted that pedestrians would be allowed to walk along the guardrails and I had no desire to test my old fear of heights. I was walking towards my goal but it looked like I was walking into a dead end.

About the time the footpath was going to evaporate it emptied into a neighborhood and business park. Hopes of a businessman's hotel rose then vanished despite the impressive and modern corporate building. The sign at the entry displayed the labels of three whiskies. Nice business, but there wasn't a sign for a tasting room. That was alright. I was tired enough that a taste or two would end my day. I wanted to do that with a bed nearby. I meandered through the neighborhood, looking for B&B signs, and asking for directions to the next town, or at least whether there was pedestrian access to the main road. The few folks I met were reticent in a now-familiar fashion. Each step was potentially a future backtrack for an exhausted me.

As I neared the far end of the houses a businessman confidently strolled up and started talking. That was a welcome surprise. He had people skills and was acting extroverted outdoors. Maybe he wasn't Scottish. He was also dressed for corporate work: dress shirt, slacks, and tasteful tie. He made sure he got out of the office for twenty minutes every day to get away from phones and emails. I shared my similar experiences from my time at Boeing. We talked for a good ten minutes, and then he extended his walk a bit more. I guess our conversation was a relief and a release from interminable work talk. He was in charge of three whiskies: Macallan, Highland Park, and The Famous Grouse, and was glad for a bit of marketing data when I told him I could get Macallan back home, but that I didn't recognize the other two. He also gave me good news. He pointed me back to the road, reassured me that it was alright to walk along it, and gave me hope that there were places to stay without having to walk twenty more miles to Dundee in what remained of the day. We had common views from different perspectives: he in the world of suits, and me walking along in my boots. You have to be active enough to get out and into the world, and then quiet enough to listen after you get there. The real world rarely visits cubicles or couches.

The day was brilliant. The dim, moist valley outside Glenfarg was replaced with autumnal T-shirt weather. I was in the land of industrial farms large enough for their own exits and crossings. Quaint vanished years ago, though a few random buildings seemed to have survived. I don't know what they harvested, but the crops grew under acres of hooped plastic covers. It looked like a Hula Hoop farm. Inside the borders, each acre was like its neighbor producing a view that changed little.

Each mile took more effort, as usual. Despite assurances, the long day turned my thoughts from sightseeing and introspection to bivouacs and contingency plans. Hope appeared as a town that was perched beside an off ramp. Without a businessman's directions I would've turned right into dense neighborhoods instead of turning left onto a frontage road that claimed two hotels. Somehow I missed the one. Was I that tired that I couldn't find a hotel along a single, short dead-end street? At least when I reached the dead-end it didn't take long to backtrack. The other place was a pub and restaurant with a detached set of rooms and a small convenience store. It was in the right place at the right time. I was tired and happy to settle in. It happened again, hot water eluded me. I could catch a cold trying to take a hot shower in Scotland.

I thought back to the businessman's walk and his useful directions. I asked for one of his whiskies so I could toast him as I sat down for dinner. They didn't have any. I was a walk away from his office. How had the man who talked about global sales and markets not managed to reach as far as his own neighborhood? The Scots drink whisky with water, not ice, but water served in a pitcher that's bigger than the glass. A little dilution I understand, but a pint of water for 70 milliliters of whisky wouldn't leave any color in the glass. I used a bit and laughed at the pitcher. The whisky may have been from another distillery, but the pitcher was from The Famous Grouse. I couldn't get the whisky but I could use their crockery. I thought about how he introduced himself and realized that he may have been President or CEO. His time was probably pricy. Had I improved his daily efficiency by more than the cost of a drink? Of course, maybe I delayed him. His hourly rate may be enough to buy a case. I joked with the waitress as I paid my bill. Of course, they had his whisky, but it was in the bar. I'd done it again. I'd seen taps and bottles and thought I was sitting where the drinkers drank, but sat in the quieter section where the food was served. Oh well, I needed the fuel more than the atmosphere.

Flipping back through my notes was entertaining. It was obvious that a country is not its tourist sites. The most memorable times were associated with natural views, rural settings, and friendly faces. No entry fee required.

I missed home. I missed cooking, a shower tall enough for me, and my electronic connectivity. I didn't miss worrying about the house, the car, and the computer. There was at least one thing I'd do different next time. A world-capable smartphone with an embedded camera would make it easier to find accommodations, stay connected, and snap shots. There'd be fewer worries and less to carry.

The land had turned greener. My plate was as brown as usual. Yep. I missed my own cooking.

It was obvious that I still hadn't exhausted the capacity to relax my thoughts. Thoughts about every topic continued, maybe heading to some resolution, and definitely keeping me from not being bored. Weeks of relaxing were successful, but plenty of tangles and swirls remained. At least each tangle and swirl was less knotted. Tension was fading.

Sprinkles started. The next day looked to be sixteen unrelenting miles into Dundee. My best hope for shortening that was to aim for the airport its possible hotels on the near side of town. That might clip a mile or two from the total, miles that are always the toughest because they come after the others.

At my room filled with modern conveniences, I put the skeleton key in the lock to open the door and chuckled at the mix of modern and historic in Scotland.

Water On My Right

October 5
Glencarse - Dundee

Rain and road noise kept me awake, and my room pointed away from the highway. Glad I didn't get a room on the front side.

By what should have been a dawn the rain abated and was replaced with overcast. That was fine by me. Sixteen miles under overcast is much better than sixteen miles in soaking rain or sixteen miles in baking sunshine. I bought cheese and candy bars as travel food. The local store didn't know about energy bars and didn't have bananas.

I'd seen few highway services so I decided to dive into the neighborhood across the overpass. I wanted plenty of places to rest, but as usual, the map only suggested a few possibilities. A more detailed map would help, but I would've spent too much time map shopping. I was between two large cities. Surely there would be restaurants. Surely there would be pubs. Surely I'd unsuccessfully tried that logic before, but my optimism is resilient.

　　　　The neighborhood went by too quickly. By the time I passed the last of the houses it was too inconvenient to backtrack to the highway. A straight sixteen miles through farm lands would be better than a total of eighteen along a sparse highway. Neither choice came with a guarantee. The road narrowed and cut straight across flat lands that were home to flocks of circling geese. Occasional bus signs were lifelines. I probably wasn't walking into a dead-end. Every grove of trees could hide a quaint collection of houses and shops. But I was in farmland and the proximity to both Perth and Dundee was only apparent when I heard or saw the highway.

　　　　And now for something completely different. Civilization had spread its culture through innovative chain saw art. Scottish versions of Easter Island statues stood facing the road. There were no plaques or signatures, but there was style and humor. It reminded me of a metal sculptor in Kansas who lined his fence posts with welded commentary. Art existed even when people weren't apparent.

　　　　Water returned! In the distance and on my right, water flowed to the North Sea. I was following the farthest reaches of the Firth of Tay. The other shore of the bay receded as the Firth widened. It was no longer a river. I'd reached an arm of the sea. Deep introspective thoughts were stored for a while. I'd reached the sea, with a bit of help from the sea reaching in towards me. My goal was near and could soon be real. Just like on the west coast, there was less of a chance of getting lost. The water would only let me go too far astray. My enthusiasm was tempered by the knowledge that all of the other sixteen miles days ended with me too tired to think. I paced my steps.

Mental introspections could be ignored for a while, but my body always demanded physical self-examinations. Every day was a different battle with my body and every day a different pain subsided. My pains were like some gang in a movie fight scene, where the bad guys decide to attack the good guy one at a time instead of as a group. I was able to manage each with different ways to wear my pack, a different stride, or different foods. Of course, the pack straps only had so many adjustments, my stride could only be so short or so long or so quick or so slow, and the foods were limited to what I could find and carry. If all my pains had hit at once I would've been stopped. Every day's new negotiation became another lesson in understanding me. My sore throat returned and was noticeable, but it didn't interfere with my progress. I repeatedly rudely cleared my throat. It would be impolite in the city but no one heard me; and if they did, I sounded far healthier than the local smokers. My aches divided into two groups: the ones from exertion and the ones from carrying stress. They were easy to mix up, but days of walking untangled them.

A sidewalk was a signal that a town approached. The opposite side was an open view across a field and down to the water. Beside me was a stone wall tall enough to block any view and straight enough to be impressive. Many stone walls were rough and sagging. This one was a mini-fortress. It welcomed me to the town of Errol, which turned out to be much larger than I'd expected. That meant it had a place to eat or stay. I had simple and easy criteria. No matter. I was there too early for either, but at least I wouldn't have to backtrack as far if nothing else showed up. My ratchet moved one notch.

I saw the pub, then I saw the church. One was blockish and visited every day. One was peaked and visited once a week. Which was more important? What would some alien think? Both involved confessions, but each story probably had at least two versions.

Errol sits a bit above the plain and the floods. On the other side of town the road flattened and straightened again and looked old. One side was bordered by a straight and evenly-spaced line of thick hardwood trees that were stronger than a guardrail. I wanted to plant seedlings between the mature trees to maintain that line for generations. Eventually they'd have to be replaced. It was the beginning of October and the leaves were still on the trees. They made for a much nicer walk and protection against too much sun. Any raindrops were delayed by their dripping travel through the leaves and branches. Either way they provided shelter.

It was hard to gauge distance except by my watch and a guess at my speed of two and a half miles an hour. On straight, flat roads, and after weeks of walking, I hoped for more progress. Farm fields flow by slowly. Landmarks and buildings were far apart and lingered on the horizon until they quickly became close and real. Then they passed and my view was replaced with another horizon and another set of imagined goals. I knew that eventually one of those goals would translate into a personal finish line, or at least a place to rest.

Not surprisingly, there was little reason for public restrooms; but, that didn't change the fact that I would need one. In a rare moment of not being able to wait any longer, I found an dense, overgrown clump of trees that looked like a bit of leftover forest instead of someone's landscaping. I wouldn't want anyone watering the bushes in my yard back home, but suburban sensibilities don't always translate beyond developer's borders. Maybe no one would ever know. Maybe no one would ever care. Rural sensibilities are different. I took one step farther to get just one more bush between me and the road, and I found myself at the back of an overgrown Quonset hut. It was camouflaged by nature. Despite my attempt at doing something natural in a natural setting, the effects of civilization were all around: the fields, the roads, and even amongst the trees. I left my mark and continued.

As the road progressed, it approached the water. Soon enough I was walking beside the Tay on a road built onto a seawall. Either the tide was in, or the rains had flooded, or both. The water was high and moving. Grasses at the base of the embankment were submerged. There was no beach or space to sit with a fishing pole. I wondered what it was like at low tide.

Water opens views. Looking miles downstream I saw a bridge that crossed the firth in sunshine. Miles behind I saw confused clouds that couldn't decide between imitating slate or coal, but they had decided on dark. Passing through one park beside a small neighborhood I met one man who said hello and actually started a conversation. That didn't last long. A few sentences later the rain began to fall. So much for a rare chat. He waved good-bye and dashed towards his house. I switched to rain gear and continued walking. The rain became a downpour.

I'd reached the edges of civilization. Sidewalks were the norm. Buses drove by, legitimizing the bus stops. The train tracks and roads came closer to parallel as the land was funneled by the encroaching shore. Airplanes on final approach were a measure of the distance to the airport. Three degree glide slopes are nearly universal. At least the rain stopped. I waited before I took off my rain gear.

Dundee's city edges became apparent with the sweep of large green lawns devoid of any sign of anyone ever walking on them. That's the nature of industrial lawns around business parks and municipal buildings. Acreage is tended as if for a garden party or a game of croquet, but if either showed up it would look out of place, and probably be chased away by the authorities. The geese should thank us. Maybe that's why they honk.

I rounded a corner and finally saw the parking lots and signage familiar to airport visitors; but, there wasn't a hotel. My expectations evaporated again. Hopes are built on assumptions. Assumptions are always suspect, even though we rely on them. They can't be ignored. But I felt silly making the same incorrect assumption again. Should I feel silly for hoping?

Dundee's airport was a nice, regional airport, large enough for most jets, but small enough to not be intimidating or noisy. One flight had just come in and left. As I walked past the lobby I got the impression that there wasn't any reason for folks to hang around so the ticket counters and lobby were empty. No wonder there wasn't a hotel. There weren't enough people.

The water that started on my left in Stranraer was now on my right in Dundee. I'd crossed Scotland on foot without much more than an idea of a route and without stepping into a car, bus, or train. What was it about me that wouldn't celebrate until I found a room for the night? The preceding miles and the late rain storm didn't help.

Finding a place to stay was a reasonable and responsible goal every day, and I am a reasonable and responsible person; so, my jubilation would be postponed until the logistics were resolved. But I knew that it occupied too much of my time. Sitting on a beach for three weeks didn't have the same daily problem. There all I'd have to do was wonder what to order and when to move from the beach to the restaurant to the bar. Staring at the same view would get boring, but maybe not. My view at home is the same every day, with variations for weather and seasons, and I'm not tired of it. I took my lack of celebration as a hint that I really wanted something else. Maybe making it to Dundee was like making it to Pensacola. The grass is always greener at the next goal, but in this case I was where the grass was green. I was simply too tired to appreciate it.

Besides, I rationalized that I'd started from lodging in Stranraer so there would be a symmetry to ending with lodging in Dundee. Would it be different if I had started walking as soon as I got off the train? Would my mental image claim the Dundee station as the logical goal, its threshold the finish line, or would I demand a return to Glasgow for closure? Goals are abstract. Celebrations are chosen by acceptance of personal definitions of success. Evidently my personal definition of success involved dinner, a drink, and a bed. I wouldn't feel successful until I found a place to stay.

A friendly litter collector saved me from my internal mental machinations. The sidewalk slid away from the road and turned into an asphalt path across the lawn. The litter picker was walking slower than everyone as he traced a jagged course from tossed coffee cup to blown bit of newspaper. We crossed paths and for a while he only picked litter within a few steps of the trail so he could have some company. He didn't know of anywhere to stay and didn't want to talk about it. He was more interested in America. He wanted to go there and see the big country. Was it dear? I've never considered America dear, though I am proud to be an American, love the people and the land, and proud of the country's history and potential. I wasn't sure what he asked about, so I told him about the parts I liked. I think he was more of a Las Vegas and road trip kind of guy. He probably wouldn't care about my favorites like hiking the Grand Canyon or climbing mountains in Washington's Cascades. At the end of the lawn he turned and went back to cover the farther flung trash. A quarter mile later I realized what he meant by dear. Dear is expensive. Depends on where you go. Depends on how you live.

The sidewalk, the shore, and the road met at an intersection that led up into the city. Into the city was into density, probably more options; but, the route along the water looked nicer. There were fewer options because only one side of the road could have buildings, but one was all I needed. A hotel along the water would feel more like reaching a goal. A hotel sunk into the city could feel like it was in the middle of something, not at an end. I wanted that feeling of crossing the goal and reaching a destination.

I enjoy watching water. I enjoy walking along water because I don't feel hemmed in. Despite that I had to walk along the other side of the road, because that's were the buildings were. I crossed the road, hoping for a sign. I'd check out the sights later, when I had dumped my gear in a room and had a beer in hand.

Instead of a hotel I found industrial walls, fences, parking lots, and superstores. Not the sort of places that received many tourists, but it was a real part of Scotland. The afternoon fading of mental resolve was familiar. Sixteen miles affected my brain as much as my body. I'd lost the reserves necessary to shop with reason, just like when I entered Glasgow. I'd probably pick the first place I found. At least the rains were replaced with blue sky.

Eventually the road peeled away from the water. The traffic swung up into the city proper but buildings squeezed into the gap between the road and the shore. I saw something that looked like a hotel. I was cautious because I'd already walked up to a few entrances to find they were the doors of municipal institutions, not hotels. At some sort of museum I saw an old tall ship and a tourism information sign. I walked into the visitor center, dramatically collapsed against their counter, and playfully appealed to them for assistance. She wasn't as dramatic. Yes, the building across the plaza was a hotel, but I couldn't just walk over there. She'd have to call first. Procedures must be followed because I'd stepped up to her counter. Politeness must be demonstrated too, but she had a job to do. Surely I'd understand. I needed the break anyway. As I leaned there, she got them on the phone, repeated the questions I would've asked, repeated the answers she heard, and then gave me some brochures and assurances about the local services. With far more information that I didn't want, and considerably less of the assistance I needed, I left after thanking her for her efforts. She meant well, was sweet, and had followed her procedures properly. Hopefully her boss would appreciate her process.

Waterfront lodging in Dundee and a sign suggesting 29 pounds a night. Maybe I'd finally found a place to relax and celebrate. Nope. The 29 pounds a night was a special online deal only available with advance notice. My room without a view would cost 82 pounds. One night sounded fine. Two nights at 82 were too much.

Another sixteen mile day and I collapsed into the room. It was nice, conventional, and could be anywhere. My view was of the parking lot. They don't vary much.

As I stripped to get ready for my shower I looked at the profile of my body. My belly bulged. I looked fat. Miles of walking and many missed meals and I was convinced I'd gained weight. Seeing my gut deflated my accomplishment. It was a familiar reaction. Fatigue and an unhealthy body image can do that. After I'd bicycled across America I felt a bit cheated. 3,800 miles, 11 weeks, and $15,000 and I didn't lose any weight, shrink my waist size, or reduce my body fat percentage. My attempt at losing weight failed. I felt like a failure. I felt like the stereotype of a middle-American with too much in the middle. It wasn't until later that I realized my criteria had nothing to do with reality. I had been healthy enough to bicycle across the North American continent. Reality was more important than any arbitrary measure based on fashion, fad, or style. I'd bicycled across a continent. Lighten up. I'd walked across Scotland. Celebrate.

The closest restaurant was forcibly designed to be modernly casual. I wanted a dinner of stereotypes: Irish Guinness, British fish and chips, and a dessert of Scottish whisky. In some restaurants, solo diners are discouraged because one person takes up as much table space and time as two, three, or four, but without spending as much money. I've been shuttled in and out of restaurants faster than in some fast food chains. These folks went the other direction. I had more than enough time to run out of things to write. I paced my Guinness. Maybe they expected me to order a second beer out of boredom. I was in a full and busy restaurant with a view of the Firth of Tay. If it wasn't for my hunger I would have been happy and content to sit there and think about what I'd accomplished. Scenery and people watching could entertain me for hours, as long as I had something to eat. Eventually food arrived after setting the record for the longest wait in Scotland. They made up for it by adding enough batter to the fish that there a palm-sized paddle firmly extending beyond the tail of the fish. Not exactly elegant. Burps arose before I was done with the main course. Dessert was cancelled. Ah, Scottish cuisine.

Congratulations on making it to Dundee. I decided to celebrate somewhere else. The coast must have lots of opportunities.

Shades Of Urban

October 6
Dundee - Monifieth

So, my stay in Dundee was expensive. The breakfast was too, but it was also small. Wait, that doesn't help. Maybe they were reacting to my reaction to my waistline. The weather encouraged me to stay. The accomplishment encouraged me to stay. The price and the food encouraged me to go. I lingered in the room, using every expensive minute there, and decided to shop for more comfortable accommodations by walking. Dundee is on the coast of the Firth of Tay. Following the Firth's shore would take me to the sea, and probably more options. I checked out after one more attempt at booking that discount rate. No luck. Off I walked.

The sad part was that the location and Dundee were just right for a relaxed day. The information booth that I visited the day before was in the foyer of a museum. I like museums. An historic sailing ship was moored outside. There were probably other attractions too. If the hotel had advertised 100 pounds and only charged me 82 without mentioning the possibility of 29 maybe I would have felt that I'd found a gem and stayed.

I decided to swing through town, walking away from the water for a while, in hopes of seeing a bit of the city and finding internet access. At a small, private postal store I checked in with my electronic and North American worlds, announcing my arrival and my new goal of Aberdeen. I'd crossed Scotland when I reached Perth, but it really wasn't by the water. I'd crossed Scotland when I reached Dundee, but it really wasn't by the sea. Reaching the sea and turning north would complete and extend my rough diagonal. I'd done what I thought I should for bragging rights and rationalization. Now I'd get to do what I wanted to do. Yet I was the one who defined it all. Whose goals were I chasing?

Wandering around Dundee was relaxing as long as I kept my bearings by keeping a watch for the water. I wandered up to a cathedral, but I only peeked inside. I quit going to church decades ago but continue to consider them someone's sacred ground, not just a tourist stop. Buildings were weathered and used, as they should be in a city. They were filled with businesses, but I wasn't going to work; and shops, but I wasn't going to buy anything. Concrete canyons cut me off from my place in the world. The horizons were too close and artificial.

It was almost lunchtime by the time I was done communicating and strolling. Breakfast had been minimal enough that thoughts of light fast food stepped to the front. Nothing appealed, not even one of my guilty pleasures: a Kentucky Fried Chicken I found after the doors were open but before they were serving. How did that happen? Maybe I talked to the wrong cashier. I wanted to see what they'd do with American Southern cuisine, but I didn't want to wait. If it was too early for eating, then it was too early for window shopping. I ambled my way out of classic downtown architecture and aimed myself at the water.

The water wasn't as obvious as the parking lots. Big box stores were busy and the lots, car parks, were filling. It felt like suburbia anywhere even though it was within a short walk of downtown Dundee. The previous day's scenic waterfront was replaced with active maritime industry. Chain link fences, railroad tracks, warehouses and terminals occupied the shore as ships and cargoes were tended. The fellow pedestrians definitely weren't tourists. Tired, grimy ship workers didn't look as friendly as tired, mud-splattered farmers. I became cautious about personal space and defensive posturing.

The transitions kept coming. Within a short while I was amongst houses again. The homes were a peaceful change from the claustrophobic city and the paved and fenced waterfront. My horizons were greener and more welcoming. I relaxed. Despite being where thousands of people lived, I walked alone as much as if I was on a rural road. People don't walk much, but they built sidewalks anyway. They might not use them, but I wouldn't turn them down.

The night's heavy rain filled puddles that the cars repeatedly tried to empty on me. The strip of landscaping between the sidewalk away from the road was enough of a buffer to keep my pants dry.

The puddles were everywhere, in the road, in the yards, but not on the bowling green. Stamped onto the local aesthetic was a tight green lawn manicured for lawn bowling. The playing area was surrounded by a drainage moat, and the moat was crossed by a small aluminum bridge. It was a landscaper's fortress. A metal gate stood in for a portcullis. A bright white painted shelter was empty and waiting for players, judges, or spectators. It was surrounded by meticulously square-trimmed hedges. Within rings of intensely managed artifacts lay very short grass waiting for people to expertly roll balls across it in intense competition. Nothing seemed casual. Everything looked orderly. Outside the hedged border was a more natural world. Puddles blocked the access. The trees threatened to drop leaves on the immaculate surface. Wind blown debris was scattered without confining itself to sidewalk, or median, or street, but the leaves were frightened enough to not fall on the lawn. I wondered if players were restricted because of weight to keep from making an impression.

Finally, a truly short day. In a welcome blessing my adventure didn't drag into a recursive two-more-miles search. I reached Monifieth, an extension of the urban corridor equipped with library, shops, and a sweet hotel and restaurant that was far more appealing and about half the price of the room I'd checked out of less than four hours earlier. I'd only traveled seven miles, possibly the shortest trip of the trip, and I'd managed to change the day from the begrudging acceptance of a hasty choice to a conscious claiming of a pleasant setting. I'd moved from what I needed to what I wanted. I checked in, ready for an early nap, a visit to the library, maybe a short walk through the shops, and maybe a mid-afternoon beverage. Cutting my mileage in half left me with enough energy to consider sightseeing. There were even a castle and a lighthouse that I could visit. First, check in, unpack, recover.

The Panmure Hotel reminded me of Glenfarg, old enough to use solid wood and have slightly warped floors under heavy carpets. Even the staircase had a sense of presentation. The stairs swept up from the registration desk as if to give the clerks a proper view of their guests ascending to the rooms. The handrail was stout and filled a hand. It was much more than some dowel rod screwed onto some posts. The richness of the wood was masculine. Paintings of men at sport marched along the walls. The building felt secure though not square. It had settled into a long existence and confidently relaxed itself into a more comfortable shape. I'd negotiated a cheaper room because an expensive room chased me out of Dundee. I found myself in a room with all of the amenities, but on a bed that felt like a small cot. I wouldn't notice that after I was asleep. The view was of a bit of hemmed-in roof, which wasn't better or worse than looking at a Dundee parking lot. At least the roof-top puddle made a good rain indicator. The weather was changing. I was glad to be indoors.

It was a rest half-day, though I finished the same time as usual because I started later than usual and electronically wandered a while back in Dundee. My wandering wasn't complete though so I strolled up to the library, pleased to find how easy it was to walk when I'd only gone seven miles instead of seventeen. Shorter days would make for a nicer though longer trip, but shorter days wouldn't always end at a place to stay. Finally I had one of those. I stayed at the library long enough to tell friends that I was alive, and to tell potential partners that I wouldn't be able to meet them for another week or so, unless they happened to be on the northeast coast of Scotland. It could happen.

The weather turned greyer, colder, and windier. I skipped the tourist sites. I reminded myself that it was a rest day, so it made sense to give my legs some time off. I did little else except sit in the hotel bar, sip and read, and wait for dinner. It wasn't dramatic, but it was appreciated. There wasn't much to write about, but such hours are the reason for many vacations.

Dinner started as a solitary event, maybe because it was autumn. I enjoyed the peace and quiet, but didn't expect it to last, especially for the hotel's sake. They needed more business than a solitary walker. About the time I was done eating my main course, the older members of a family came in and filled a table. My dinner had been quiet reading but my dessert was served with boisterous eavesdropping. They had more than a sherry or two, and the sherries worked better than counseling. Everyone jumped in and out of arguments and ended up laughing. How did they do that? I'd never witnessed such emotional openness, resilience, and willingness to communicate loudly and without diplomacy or politeness. They got a lot out, and then let it go by. Their emotional health probably surpassed mine. Every culture has its good points, and I got to witness some of Scotland's.

Obvious eavesdropping is impolite so, even though I enjoyed their true life drama, I decided to retire to a comfy chair in the bar to drink another dessert and read. My room was small enough that I didn't want to hide there. A few pages later a work party, home from their shift, came in and replayed a similar scene: boisterous, argumentative, and laughing. Fun again, but after a while I retreated to my cot and relaxed with my eyes closed.

Realization seeped in. After college I became the sort that didn't blend at bars. I don't cheer when crossing the finish line because it's never felt as if the race has been won. What happened back there and then to temper my celebrations? Most of my adventures, journeys, projects, and goals are large or long. Bicycling across America was not a sprint. Neither is walking across Scotland, writing a book, tackling five-year-long photography essays, or learning karate. I'll probably cheer when I win the lottery jackpot. I'd probably cheer more often if there was someone to cheer with. On my own though, celebrations are usually quiet smiles and a good meal. I was glad that I could embrace contentment, but saddened that I skipped celebration.

I'd rested. It felt good, and hopefully it would make it easier to reach Aberdeen. It was the classic pacing dilemma. Each hour spent in one place effectively made each remaining day longer. But pushing too hard for too long could mean burning out and not reaching my goal. Aberdeen was a goal that barely fit inside my flight schedule. A couple of extra days might make the trip much more enjoyable, but also that much more expensive. The stock market had not been kind to me while I was gone. I could move the flight or the goal, but decided not to move either. I'd move me.

Welcome To The Coast

October 7
Monifieth - Arbroath

A gorgeous morning. Golf courses look best just after dawn, and the hotel was equipped with fairways, greens, and early golfers walking across the dew. My scrambled eggs waded across the plate. That's one way to get fluids for the day. The peacefulness of the course was shaken as commuter trains rumbled by. The people on the way to work got to watch the people who had the day off.

I only saw one freight train. It was fifteen cars long, not even practice for the mile-long trains that cross America.

Fog filled the air and shrunk the world to grey walled vignettes. My route would be a series of guesses based on views that ended at a quarter mile. My morning had short horizons.

I intended to stay between the highway and the coast, and guessed that the bicycle network would have the same idea. I was right. There were trail signs but when I tried to follow them I got lost. I'd think I was on the trail, but then bump into the highway. Then I'd make a guess, take a turn, and walk. After a while I'd find another sign that pointed me to the trail. Trail signs led back onto side roads. I'd lose the trail, steer back to the highway, and re-find the trail. The trail signs seemed like a lot of detours to make sure tourists wandered the empty countryside getting thirsty enough to drain a keg at the next pub.

During one attempt to chase down the trail a lesson showed up with the sound of hammers. I came across a hotel that probably showed up in guidebooks: rooms and food along a vacant bit of road. Maybe I would've steered towards it if I'd planned an itinerary, because it was just a little bit farther and I tended to steer towards a bit more progress. Two men were hammering plywood across the windows and doors. The place had been out of business long enough to grow impressive weeds. Rodents would make sure it wasn't completely vacant. Businesses come and go but live forever in print. Of course, sometimes they pop up when needed, like back in Fossoway; and that one was too new to show up in a guide. Maybe a lack of planning was as effective as a meticulous itinerary.

The countryside was mega-farms split by the highway. There was green in those fields. It never seemed to end up on my plate, but they obviously grew it. Hoop farms re-arose too. Half-hoops slinkied across the fields, usually barren and brown from the recent harvest, but sometimes draped in acres of plastic. Crops were highly protected, but against what? Wind? Hailstorms? Locusts? The fields were large and flat enough to accommodate factory-size equipment. The economies of scale were at work, which meant I saw no workers. Automation happens, or the people hid under the plastic.

My mini-day of rest was followed by doubts and negative thoughts. The feeling was the same that I got from eating food containing wheat or gluten, but I couldn't recall accidentally having any of that. Maybe bad moods just happen. Maybe good moods just happen. I was hoping for Indian Summer, and wondering about which Indian it referred to. A bit of warmth would've helped. The days were cold but not crisp. It wasn't a dry cold, but a marine cold, with humidity carrying heat from my body. The days were noticeably shorter. Maybe that was it.

For a while the trail steered away from the water, but by lunchtime the fog lifted. The horizon brightened as light glared off the North Sea. I was back by the water in the town of Elliot, which was sprouting a mini-garden of big-box stores and fast food joints. MacDonald's was open, ready and busy. The KFC would join it in a week or so, too late for me. I got an order of chicken to go from MacDonald's, sat outside to keep from odiferously offending the parents and children, poured a large drink into me, and then hopped across lawns to find the sidewalk again. My lunch wasn't as enjoyable as fish and chips, but that local staple wasn't popular enough to inspire a chain of stores, so I had to resort to American Standard.

Elliot was closer to Arbroath than I expected. I'd quickly walked from rural to suburban to urban. Out of habit I walked to the waterfront looking for a hotel. They were there, but they reminded me of the pub in Denny: as in lock the door and don't touch anything. It was my mistake. Arbroath has a working waterfront. The lodging was for mariners and served up a different set of niceties. The niceties that I wanted were probably in places up in town, a few blocks away from the water. I was learning. The Ogston Hotel had a restaurant and a sidewalk sign. I spotted them both and stopped shopping. It was only about 1PM and I'd already walked 12 miles. The next town looked much farther along the coast, about another day's journey. I was finally gauging my pace. It had only taken two weeks for me to learn that about myself too.

The hotel didn't have a laundry, but the manager knew where to find one. He gave me directions that led me on a tour of the town. I'd get to do three things at once: walk more, play tourist, and get clean clothes.

It would have been a relief to walk through town, browsing through stores, maybe stopping for a pint out of novelty's sake, but I was on a mission and carrying a load. The laundry was about a half mile away through a series of disjointed directions. The street grid was built to accommodate wharfs, piers, and water centuries ago. It felt like a square grid that was laid on land that subsequently flowed. Turn left or turn right was replaced with bear left and bear right and swing around this one corner and look for the street that heads off a bit around a particular building. I wanted to flow my way over to the laundry, but wondered if I would swirl off and get lost. Laundries are not major landmarks. Somehow it worked. When I finally got there I realized it would've been easier to get directions to its neighbor, the railway station.

What I found was one woman, a lot of machines, all of which she was operating, and great chaos. She was a single mom amidst a rush. Adding me wasn't going to help, but my clothes needed her services. Her kid needed her too. A child's emergency pulled her to some unexpected meeting in the middle of the day. I walked in as she was getting ready to walk out. She assured me that she'd try to get my clothes cleaned before dinner, but I'd have to wait somewhere else because she had to lock the shop.

Ah, a forced opportunity to venture about. I dropped the idea of dropping in for a pint because the pubs looked more menacing than inviting. The patrons smoking at the doors gave me territorial glances, as if they were the gatekeepers to private parties. The shops were friendlier, but they were like Hollywood storefronts, decorated yet vacant. I feel for shop owners who have to maintain a pleasant persona while politely entertaining browsers who treat their shops as museums and displays instead of businesses. I didn't want to waste their time. Besides, most of them were selling things made somewhere else. There was no reason to Buy Scottish if it was Made In China. I didn't want to spend a couple of hours bumping my way through aisles full of things I wouldn't buy.

An internet cafe wasn't high on my list, but I dropped in anyway because it was familiar, cheap, and a proven way of wasting a lot of time without spending a lot of energy. It was also a window on modern reality. It was more of a computer services store than a cafe, and had more traffic than the other shops. There were a couple of computers for rent. I sat on a stool and browsed electrons. He stayed behind the counter and tended to hardware and software problems that customers lugged in the door. I had more privacy than in libraries or hotel kiosks. No one was looking over my shoulder. Talking to the owner and people watching were more entertaining than anything online. He had experience and no degree, and kept a busy business by continuing to learn and by treating most people with respect. There are always a few that make unreasonable requests, and computers can produce many examples of "It should do this, but it did that instead." Of course, a computer is never unreasonable. It always acts completely rationally, but they are complicated enough that guessing the rationale and the reasoning are no longer simple. Sounds a lot like trying to understand people.

After a while I decided to be brave and spend some time in the pub closest to the laundry, but along the way I found something much better and completely different: a salad bar. I didn't realize how much I craved greens until I walked in and saw what they were serving. The thought of eating something that wasn't brown was intoxicating. The salads looked good, very good. I ordered a hard cider, which turned out to be harder than I expected, and a plate of greens, which was never so appreciated. My body jumped in. The pity was that they were closing before the laundry opened. The space was light, friendly, and comfortable. I could've happily sat there reading a book and drinking another cider, but they had a closed sign and knew how to use it. They had lives too.

The laundry was still closed. Luckily, the weather was fine for autumn, warm in the sunshine, chilly in the shade. I checked in at the train station, making sure of schedules and rates in case I found myself heading back to Glasgow unexpectedly. It was really just an excuse to waste some time. The sun felt great when I stepped outside. I'd walked enough. What I really wanted was to sit and relax. What I wanted was right beside me. The station's stone front was hard, but had soaked up sun all morning. I sat with my back as flat against the wall as possible so the warm stone heat massaged me. Maybe I looked like an indigent because my seat was on the sidewalk. No one threw coins my way. The only people that noticed me were teenagers. I think I was sitting in the middle of their unofficial version of a skateboard park.

I was waiting at the laundry when the owner returned. She was tired and ready for the end of the day, with one child's crisis behind her but with hours of work before her. I thanked her for her effort, wished her well, and got out of her way. With laundry hung over my shoulder I walked back to the hotel. Health food and a warm stone massage weren't enough to revive my feet enough for an extended walking tour of the town. It was dusk, most businesses were shutting down, and I was hungry.

My hotel room was comfortable. The bar was modern. The restaurant had good food and personable service. The manager actually seemed to care about the needs of a walking tourist from The States, with the little time a busy host could provide. Everything considered, Arbroath was a fine package for a place to stay. I'd finally found a place with everything I wanted, just as I found myself wanting and believing that I could make it to Aberdeen. I wanted more than I could have.

My flight out was less than a week away, and it looked like it would take a little less time than that to get to Aberdeen. The trip started with a goal based on a personal need that was burdened with self-imposed peer pressure. I needed an active vacation, but by picking a challenging goal I opened the possibility of looking like a liar or a quitter. That attitude started changing before I got to Glasgow. My needs and wants were increasingly more important than the stories or achievements. My desire to reach Aberdeen was mine. My friends hadn't changed. They'd never imposed any pressure. They'd accept me regardless of what I did. I was stepping beyond my imagined needs for social acceptance and walking into my personal world.

The next few days would be a walk along the coast, which was the way I started the trip, but it became a pull instead of a push.

I lingered a bit over dinner, watched the tables fill with urbanites, and went to bed early.

Foggy Horizons

October 8
Arbroath - Montrose

The forecast was for clear and 70 degrees, except where I was. The rest of the British Isles were going to have warm and sunny. My edge of the North Sea was packaged with fogs, mists, and chills. My head wanted to sit and watch the world go by. My muscles and pack-pinched nerves agreed. My organs felt best with lots of nice, light exercise. I wanted to walk to Aberdeen. The votes were counted. I packed and walked into a foggy morning.

The hotel manager described the coast as a long stretch of little harbor towns. He made it sound like a day of pub hopping. The scenic trail supposedly followed the water. Harbor towns, pubs, and scenery made a nice package. The fog completed the setting for a stereotypical Scottish walk.

As always, town faded quickly. Cities exist within small boundaries. It took more time to walk off breakfast than it did to walk out of town. Soon enough the trail led me to an expansive park sandwiched between a brick-walled neighborhood and a receded sea. I was surprised it wasn't a golf course. Low tide exposed broken black rocks. Early morning dog walkers slowly explored the uneven terrain. They were dressed for foul weather. Life jackets looked more appropriate. The horizon lived at the edge of the fog.

Beyond the nearly empty park the land spread out towards a promontory on the right and into farmland on the left. The trail headed to the promontory, which was probably scenic and inside a cloud. The trail marker suggested that chance of scenery came at the price of an extra three miles. Three mile detours might be resented if the end of the day stretched out too far. Steering straight was the safer bet, and besides, the fog ate the seascape. The ocean views would be truncated as long as the mist prevailed. I knew my goal, but didn't know how I was going to get there. I also knew any choice was bounded by out of sight borders: the highway far to my left, and the sea far to my right. I aimed for the middle and what I hoped would be the shortest path.

That didn't last long. The road quickly became the entrance to a farm and a walled compound with signs for "No Trespassing", "No Visitors", "Do Not

Enter." Maybe they posted all three signs. I can't remember because I wasn't taking notes, but I knew I wasn't welcome. The fog made the place feel like a Scottish version of some sci-fi movie. I needed and wanted directions, and there was nowhere else to find them; so, there was no reason to hide the fact that I was in the wrong place. I walked straight towards the mobile office: a trailer set in the parking lot. Its lights were on and I heard the familiar sound of a morning staff meeting breaking up. People were shuffling around. Maybe a chair scraped the floor. When I was about twenty feet away a few of the fellows came out, headed for their tasks. Their boss came out too. Before he had a chance to tell me to leave I called out that I was lost and wanted to know the best way to get off their land. Everyone else kept going, except for the boss and another guy. They came my way and gruffly told me that I should get a good map. I said he was right and that I was a fine example of what happens when a tourist uses a bad map. He laughed. Hallelujah. There was a side lane, not even a road, that skirted the property. I'd seen it and wondered if it was the best way back to the highway. Yep. He'd rather have me walk there instead of trying to make it across his massive factory farm. They gave me some directions which made no sense, but I had permission to skirt the property, so I skirted.

     The lane was uneven, muddy, and obviously used by big-wheeled farm equipment. I suspected that the farmhands didn't walk much. The place was too big. It was impressive walking past that much hooped and plastic-sheltered cropland. If I didn't know about the inevitable highway I would have thought that their directions were leading me into wilderness, but I was in Scotland, not Wyoming. The lane ended at an innocuous road that definitely wasn't the highway. I only had two choices, besides backtracking, so I turned right and hoped that my diagonal hadn't turned into a day of zig-zags.

The fog filtered the scene with wonderful light. Silhouettes of trees and stone walls receded into vanishing perspectives. Mist draped across everything like a very heavy dew, but it wasn't enough to warrant rain gear. The pavement was sometimes covered in mud, frequently rough, and rarely equipped with painted stripes. Maybe the stripes were there, but under inches of mud. Instead, the lanes were defined by autumn's debris. A brown line of broken leaves marked the middle of the road. Two more marked the edges. I was alone. There were no herds of cattle or flocks of sheep to accompany me. Recently harvested fields were turned earth with stubble left as a hint of what had grown there. The farmers were probably somewhere warmer and drier.

There are advantages to being alone and lost in the fog. The lack of visibility and the old, low, stone walls suggested some privacy for getting rid of the morning's tea. I stepped around a waist high wall, and onto a field behind a bush and still felt nervous. I was sure that a tour bus would drive up as soon as I unzipped.

Maybe I was lost. There was no way to tell. There weren't any trail signs, and the intersections weren't marked, or were marked with names that had no meaning to me or my map. I wasn't too worried. It was a beautiful morning. My camera got a workout. My progress slowed as I set myself against trees and walls to steady otherwise shaky shots in the low light. I could've spent the entire day photographing one lane with a few gnarled trees. Their leaves covered the field at their feet and a bit of the road. Their branches were sculpted by decades of wind. What remained were their arms perennially reaching and readying for the next season. They were equipped to survive the winter because they gave up what they no longer needed in the expectation that they could make the leaves again.

It was unnerving, walking along a signless road, a road very much less-traveled. Intersections happened, as much to mark field boundaries as to provide options for travelers. I never knew if I should turn or go straight, but I kept a straight line because there was no obvious reason to change. If I found the highway, I'd feel secure. If I found the sea, I'd enjoy the sights and hope it wasn't a dead end. If I was lucky enough, I'd find a town where the highway and the sea met. That one possibility of a dead end was the only cause for concern. Listening to clues was frustrating. The background noise was a constant, deep rumble with a few high notes that could either be tire noise, waves on the shore, or wind through nearby, high, unseen trees. If I was walking to a little harbor town, the little harbor town must get most of its traffic through the harbor because there wasn't much on the road. I began to suspect I was walking towards a desolate, beautiful, and spartan seaside park.

Foggy pastures, uncertain destinations, personal isolation, are not the selling points in a travel brochure, but they made for a beautiful day of walking. I relaxed into the quietude of the day. My horizons were simple and visually poetic. Sculpted trees, and patterned fields. Leaves skittering across the road, and branches creaking as they let the wind blow through. No demands. No expectations. No historical markers to memorize or past deeds that asked for ritualistic respect. I was alone in the world and the world was fine. We accepted each other.

Eventually, the day's background soundtrack revealed itself to be the nearby hidden ocean, but instead of a dead-end I found an intersection of pavement and the sea. I was lucky enough to find a town where the highway and sea meet: Ferryden, a mariner's town. It felt odd walking amongst buildings again. The sky had darkened as if it were dusk, but it was only mid-afternoon. The houses, the traffic, industrial buildings, even the sidewalks and street hemmed me in after my walk through the universe that was fields fading into fog; but I relaxed because I'd reached civilization before dark. The fields were expansive and suggested freedom. The city was probably expensive and promised comfort. How about some inexpensive, expansive comfort?

The highway crossed an arm of the sea via a bridge over a major inlet. On the other side was the much larger city of Montrose. They were all just dots on the map until I walked up to them. Ferryden was a street or two. Montrose was a network of streets, alleys, and service roads. Walking fourteen miles in a fog can make any sign of civilization seem like Oz. Montrose looked like a metropolis.

The inlet was wide enough for major ships, but the bridge wasn't high enough and didn't include a drawbridge, so I guessed the inlet wasn't very deep. Maybe small powerboats could get through. The tide was coming in and filling a basin that would have been an excellent harbor if it was deep enough. The debris and the navigation markers were severely swept by an powerful tidal flow. I wonder if the basin emptied to mud at low tide, like Cultus Bay does back home. Watching the water was an excuse for a rest. I needed it. I wanted it. I enjoyed it. Hotel shopping was simple when there was only one choice, or too tiring if I had to make choices after a long day. Montrose looked big enough to have lots of options. I wanted to be rested enough to check out more than one. I also enjoyed watching the tide come in. Currents are even more impressive when I envision them as flowing out of a pipe and into an empty basin. Nature uses enormous pumps that never break. I spent a few extra minutes on the bridge watching the sea fill the land.

Montrose was arranged as I expected for an old town, a main road through the middle where a plaza opened into a space that looked ready for an open-air market. But it was in Scotland, so the plaza was bordered by solid stone buildings that suggested that any open-air market would only happen with lots of weather protection for the goods and the people. A couple of churches added their weight to the space and I steered around each hunting for room signs.

Opening onto the long, double-wide plaza was an establishment that looked convenient and well-kept. It was so convenient that I imagined getting a room there, and then wandering around the shops for the afternoon, though my legs had a way of vetoing excursions after remembering how good it felt to sit. Their signs led me into a less-agreeable alley and up a flight of stairs to the front desk. The clerk, or maybe the owner, saw me before I saw them. They were ready to quickly tell me that they were full and that every bed in town was booked. My optimism threw up its hands. This did not sound good. They gave me the name of another hotel which involved backtracking and a detour, and told me not to get my hopes up.

I passed empty storefronts which weren't encouraging and then around a corner I saw a well kept building and a sign: The George Hotel. It looked nicer than the other place, though small. But as I walked in it grew and continued to impress me. The clerk was friendly despite being very busy. Yes they had a room. It was upstairs in the far back corner and one of the last in the place. They gave me directions that seemed as contorted as the ones I needed to find the hotel. The stairway had character. It twisted and spiraled without recognizing vertical or horizontal. My guess was that sometime the ground had shifted beneath the building. Instead of worrying about it, the owners simply shrugged and continued operating because it hadn't fallen over. The warps turned the landings into banked corners. Up the stairs, onto the landing, turn to the other stairs, through the other door, down the hall, around the corner and there I was, my own skinny room. I dropped my pack, sat on the bed, and listened as my legs told me that they didn't want to get up. I wasn't surprised. I took care of myself and then took care of my gear.

Eventually I wandered the long trip downstairs and found a gem. They had a computer for guests. Score!

Score was right. The computer was across the six foot lobby from the front desk cubby. Someone was using computing power superior to the Apollo Program to watch a soccer game. I wanted to use all of that computing power to talk to my friends. Negotiations were pleasantly concluded. They could always rewind to the good parts and I wouldn't take long. Besides, it was soccer, maybe the score wouldn't change in the meantime.

Computers remember. Start typing an address into a browser and it may guess at where you are going. My friends and my home were on Whidbey Island. As I typed Whi the computer filled in the rest. Someone from Whidbey had been there. Sitting beside the computer was a stack of donated books. One of the books was written by Elizabeth George, a writer who lives on Whidbey. I was in The George Hotel. The computer, the books, and the hotel name all started to sound like some Hollywood setup. Even though Whidbey is effectively a small town I had not met the highly esteemed Ms. George. I wondered if she'd been there. Maybe we could compare notes. Maybe we could carpool and I could return to Montrose. Nah.

After my stint with the computer I settled into their restaurant for an early beer, a bit of reading, and an early dinner. Early dinners were especially welcome when I missed lunch. Quiet countrysides are appealing, but left me hungry. Anything they served would be marvelous, and the first beer into a tired body made me much more receptive. The late afternoon dinner crowd was like back in America, mostly elderly and set in their habits. Everyone probably knew their places. By the time I finished my meal the average age was dropping towards drinking age and the noise level was rising towards boisterous. The rooms were full because the next day was a soccer match between Montrose and Stranraer.

Finally I had a refresher course in how to pronounce the place where I'd started. It was raer, not rear. I'd been saying Stran rear, like the back end of the Stran, whatever that was. Raer was pronounced differently. It didn't make any more sense, but at least the locals finally understood me.

Every table filled and then a crowd piled in. People gravitate to noisy places. Is it to get lost in the noise? Would a lonely, noisy celebration somehow be too sad? Is it to drown out inner thoughts? I steer to the quiet so I can hear myself and the world, but sometimes I need innocuous noise to sleep. Maybe some people use noise to never wake up. Whatever the reason, they sounded like they were having fun.

Lasagna and chips for dinner. Odd and welcome, like my quiet room up the twisted staircase that removed me from the shouts and the party.

Harbor Towns

October 9
Montrose - Inverbervie

Nice town. Nice hotel. Nice time for a break, but then I wouldn't make it to Aberdeen. My preference for sitting, writing, and reading lost to my desire to reach my goal. I could write later.

My route fell away from highways and rail lines quickly. Instead, I followed a little coastal road that only had Saturday driver traffic. There were fewer trucks, but many more cars. People exercising their fancy cars on slick roads meant my dance along the shoulder was more energetic. The big trucks may lean in the corners, but professional drivers are cautious. Saturday drivers were releasing a workweek's frustrations by busting out of their office life and stressing their cars across a land without cubicles. They were escaping one world by blasting past its borders. I gave them as much room as possible.

I watched the world from a slower and quieter perspective.

Autumn was obvious. Leaves were plastered to pavement. Hedges were fringed in temporary brown. The lighting was subdued and only reluctantly reached the ground. Tourist brochures show blue sky, sunny days. The right overcast can be very appealing. A bright overcast meant no distracting glare, but intense colors. Yellow didn't fade to brown. There was a sharp-edged difference between the day's vibrant display and the previous week's detritus. Old leaves died, dried, and fell in waves. Rose hips stayed and added red accents that stood out redder than the flower that preceded them. The leaves were gone, isolating the bud of color with space and easily overlooked branches.

The coast reached in via a tributary that required tall bridges: one old, one older. The road followed one. The other was weathered, leaf-covered and built for a railroad, but the rails were gone and the grading paved for pedestrians. The bridge was high and long so the railroad could jump from one bit of hill across a wide stream and over to the opposite hill. The power of water to cut through a hill was easy to overlook, but impressive after it was noticed. At some point the two hills may have been connected as one ridge. An entire hill had been washed out to sea by a stream of water much smaller than what it moved. Humans then came along, found a new source for rocks, and piled them up into a bridge. I took my time enjoying the sights from dozens of feet above the water, safe from traffic and only left with the remnants of my fear of heights. I felt privileged that so much structure was there merely to allow a couple hundred pounds of person to walk across water.

Old bridges impress me. Anything standing after a hundred years, especially after being heavily used, has outlived people and generations. In contrast, much of modern life is temporary. Would a modern bridge, designed by architects under the influence of committees, public debate, and municipal funds last as long? The rail bridge, and then the road bridge when I looked back, carried more character and looked readier to survive longer than long metal spans supported by dozens of steel cables. Architects must have been involved back then too. Maybe they had just as many constraints, but also had to deal with displeasing royalty and possibly losing their head instead of a contract. Decapitation can motivate overdesign and large factors of safety which just happen to lead to longevity for the bridge and its designer. Maybe it was newer than I knew, but the damp day made it look ancient.

I'd finally fallen into a groove, a new rut for each day's walk. A bit more than two weeks were all it took to develop a new set of habits that I could sustain as well as any other rut. At a guess, it would only take a bit more than my normal annual living expenses to continue for a year. I did some math as I walked and realized that my mortgage payment was approximately the same as paying for a hotel room, and the hotel takes care of the maintenance instead of me. Food on the road was more expensive, but walking drastically reduced the amount of stuff that needed maintaining and tending. Cardiovascular health would improve, though joints might be a bit more worn eventually. Mental health would definitely be better, but there would be a lack of community if there wasn't companionship. I had a new understanding of nomads and gypsies.

Despite that numbers game and thoughts of constant wandering, I looked forward to being home. Memories of my shower, my bed, my community, and cooking my own meals took me out of the moment. I liked my life. Sometimes I simply needed to step away from it for a while to see it properly.

While I distracted myself I didn't notice the land I passed through. I've seen other tourists do the same thing. There's a difference between being here or there. We are always here, wherever that is. There is someplace else. Travelers go from here to there, but when they arrive, they have a new here. But not always. People from the city visit the country and try to keep it at arm's length. Country folk visit the city and can't fit in. I'd seen it happen when I was camping at Merritt Lake, as part of writing my book about the lake. The leader of a group walked up to the lake and announced to his group, "We're there!" Evidently not. Some part of him was still back in the car, and probably back home.

Living on a touristy island proved to me that most tourists aren't here. They are there. It is common for someone on vacation to see themself removed and somewhat distant from their surroundings, carrying a bubble of their other life with them. The bubbles are reinforced by staying inside metal boxes and tubes like cars and planes. I wasn't immune. I didn't exactly jump into pubs every night and become one of the locals, but I also didn't hide myself in the shell of a car. Bicycling and walking put me into the world that I traveled through. Though, my mind regularly drew me away to an internal bubble. By realizing that I missed part of the trip, I noticed my own transition from here to there and back again. It made me appreciate how much I appreciated my trip.

Johnshaven had the right name. It included the word haven, and maybe it could live up to it, but I knew that making it to Gourdon or Inverbervie would make it easier to make it to Aberdeen. Each goal affected the next. Besides, it was Saturday; maybe the library wouldn't be open. I let the town slip by with some regret.

The road climbed away from the water. Maybe the coast had enough rocks, ravines, and cliffs to discourage wave-hugging highway and railway construction. Straighter has its advantages when trying to connect the dots. Any scenic side roads were going to be skipped. I wasn't going to detour down potential dead ends. Backtracking cost two times too much.

Down by the water the houses were modest and looked like the homes for farmers and workers. As the road rose it passed bigger homes that looked like mansions and manor houses. They were higher, back from the water, maybe for the view, or maybe to get away from corrosive salt spray. Waterfront sells well in the States, but Scotland's relationship with the sea looked more adversarial. The North Sea is known for storms and the dangerous life of fishing and shipping. There was less of a tendency to elbow forward for a front row seat.

Walking an empty road past isolated estates on a grey autumn day took me back to horse and carriage days. Groceries and visitors had a long way to go. Every trip had some adventure included. I pitied the poor draft animals. The ridgetop houses were exposed to great views and foul weather. The few remaining trees acted as climate gauges of the strength and direction of the prevailing winds. Even on a calm day there'd be a desire to lean into the wind. The isolation and the climate would be easy to ignore from inside a comfortable car that could travel to the next city in under an hour.

The road was a highway, but without many cars. I fell into a quiet, almost meditative rhythm. But every car was an interruption. A blast of noise, a look over my shoulder to make sure I was safe, and a doppler shifted rumble as the car sped past me. Wait a few minutes and repeat, after a momentary return to quiet contemplation. I relaxed in the gaps and patiently waited for the traffic to pass out of sight and sound. After each car I'd notice the irritants like litter, puddles, or enormous signs that I had to duck under or steer around. People may be drawn to noise of cities, but I retreat from noise, unless I am making it. I'd return to my own world and sing or talk as I pleased. The cattle seemed to enjoy the company and followed me as far as they could.

The road stayed high, which gave me a nice view out to a storm covered sea. Breakers hit the coast as the tide came in. It must be impressive during a true storm, though a strong storm probably also obscured the view with wind-driven clouds and blasted rain. I walked under overcast and a threat of mist, relatively good weather.

Eventually a harbor town appeared on the horizon and off the highway. As I got closer the road signs confirmed that it was Gourdon. It looked big enough to have a pub, but it was also small enough to make me cautious about dead end detours. Optimism encouraged me to watch for hotel signs. Pessimism kept in mind other plans. After a while I realized that I couldn't even find an intersection that led to the town. It looked like I was going to walk past it. Was it a town only reachable by water? I doubted that. A couple of times I turned around to see if I'd spaced out and walked past a turn-off, but no. It looked like the only entrance was from the far end of town.

The design of the harbor intrigued me. I live in a much smaller neighborhood with a much smaller marina where almost every boat is a pleasure craft. Our waters are a protected bay within the protection of Puget Sound. The mouth of our marina is almost a hundred miles from the Pacific Ocean. Whitecaps happen, but they're rare. Gourdon's harbor has fortress seawalls defending against the persistence and immediacy of the North Sea. My marina's seawall is a picket fence in comparison. Within Gourdon's harbor is another harbor, with a locked inner gate probably there to keep boats afloat at low tide. It was an impressive structure. I imagined my neighborhood association trying to implement something similar simply to keep the keels straight as the tide drains the boat basin. The complexity is more than I'd like to pay for, yet here was a town that built one out of necessity, and had to build it at low tide when it wasn't storming. Tough work.

By the time I found the turn to Gourdon I was only a mile or two from Inverbervie. Walking into Gourdon meant backtracking about a half mile downhill with the possibility of having to walk back uphill if I didn't find a place to stay. Inverbervie was nearly the same distance and a much larger town. Aiming for Gourdon and missing it, made it easier to reach Inverbervie. Missing one goal can lead to attaining another. Luckily, both destinations were downhill because both were by the water. I was done climbing for the day.

Inverbervie was broader, more open, and appeared to be newer. I followed the main road, hopeful as usual, and feeling more confident as I walked into town. My was short because very soon I saw the other side of town. Maybe it was a working town and no one ever visited them. Finally I spotted an inn and a pub. The fear of the one in Denny remained, but I knew I was going to try it because I saw no other choice. I met a jovial and busy host who was surprised to see anyone. For 39 pounds I got a suite as large as the room in the renovated farm house in Fenwick, with a bed big enough for me, room enough to spread everything out, and with a pub and restaurant downstairs. Give me an extra day and I'd stay. Give me two and that would do too. The only downside was the lack of a shower. Hosing myself off European style has never been graceful. If I stand, I'm tall enough that the spray goes everywhere. If I sit, I rarely find a tub long enough. Folding my body to fit a tight, iron confine is not relaxing. I got wet and dried off and maybe got cleaner.

I definitely got relaxed. By the time I woke from my nap most of the shops were closed. My mini-tour of town was abandoned. Window shopping is cheap, but the weather encouraged me to stay indoors.

Dinner was beef, potatoes, veggies, Guinness and whisky, and a book. It was an appropriate indulgence. Laughter swept through from the bar across the hallway, which warmed the atmosphere. I was happy where I was, enjoying my own version of a fine evening.

I could stay three or four days in Inverbervie for the cost of my one day stay in Glasgow. No wonder I'm not a city guy.

Just Keep Walking

October 10
Inverbervie - Portlethen

Staring at the map, trying to read terrain and accommodation possibilities from dots and squiggles, I convinced myself that if Aberdeen has urban sprawl and a suburban fringe, then I might make it to the edge of Aberdeen in a day. That would give me an extra day in Glasgow before I flew home. The possibility enticed me into waking up early. I reached the restaurant as they unlocked the door and flipped on the lights. Eggs and bacon and orange juice for breakfast please. He paused. Why did I want oysters for breakfast? I didn't ask for oysters. I asked for orange juice. Oysters? Orange juice. Two tries later he understood my foreign accent when I pantomimed drinking the order. They served eggs and bacon on toast with a side of toast, and a glass of orange juice.

I liked the place. The placemats were made of wood, slate, or leather, sturdy materials that wouldn't be thrown away after one customer. They were there to stay.

I wondered what the town was like when the sun shone. The sky was a rainless grey. The rest of Great Britain had a forecast of clearing weather, except for northeast Scotland. Maybe I should have walked across Ireland.

Large bridges cross small streams. I didn't realize the town was so high above sea level until I reached the bridge out of town. It is a massive concrete structure that jumps from the town's plateau to the neighboring hill. Its foundation authoritatively buried an older, much narrower bridge that may have carried trains or carts. Now it only carries pedestrians, unless trains or carts are able to climb stairs. The old bridge runs into the footing of the new bridge and a stairway makes up the difference.

Before I crossed, I stepped aside to a small park with a bold sculpture. It was a monument to the clipper ship the Cutty Sark, which most folks only know about from the whisky. The figurehead of the ship was displayed bare-breasted. Her weathered bosom may authentically replicate the ship and history, but in the present it probably had more of an influence on adolescent boys. It was nice to see that the town was proud of being the birthplace of the ship's designer. Too many towns spend more time idolizing rich athletes.

Crossing the bridge brought me closer to the city of Aberdeen, but it was a quick transition back to no shoulder. As usual I danced the day away hopping from certain progress on asphalt to tentative steps over uneven ground. The road curved up and away from town and people. My steps were uncertain but my goal was clear. I walked across rolling headlands with occasional, long glimpses to rocky cliffs and big waves. Or maybe it was all mirages in the clouds. The trail signs were there again and I tried to follow them, but I'd lose the trail, find it, lose it, and find it. Eventually I decided to ignore the signs. It saved me time and effort, and I ended up intersecting it anyway. Following someone else's route wasn't as relaxing as choosing my own path and being lost occasionally. I probably missed sights that tourism bureaus thought needed to be seen, but I undoubtedly saw sights that most people never noticed. Luckily, I am easily pleased.

I dreamed of Aberdeen but I aimed for Stonehaven. It was the next dot on the map, and probably had tourist facilities because it had a little tourist information i next to it on the map. Finding security was always calming. Walking past an inn reset my comfort zone and the distance I'd have to backtrack if something went wrong. Besides, maybe I'd like Stonehaven enough to redefine my goal, declare success and stay there until my train ride back to Glasgow and the airport.

It must have been a meditative morning. I was so relaxed and in the groove of walking, that most of the morning went by without a note. Which was more important: remembering every detail so I could legitimize my trip by telling lots of stories when I got back, or embracing the moment so well that the next moment chased out the memory of the previous moment in a continual cycle? I was walking. I was enjoying my life. Should anything else matter on vacation? Should anything else matter in life? The advantage of vacation is not worrying about responsible thoughts like bills, maintenance, and planning for the future. Miles drifted by and I was finally in a frame of mind that was enjoyable and therapeutic. Now I was ready to go on vacation because I could enjoy it instead of should it.

As a writer and a speaker I've learned that five seconds of a mis-adventure can be a richer story than five hours of meditative calm. One time at Lake Valhalla I found myself upside down in a tree well. It was easy to write about my mis-step, the fall, the hanging from my snowshoes, the careful releasing of the buckles, and the subsequent drop and slide into pine needles and mud, and the thoughts that went through my mind. Five hours of sitting beside Lake Valhalla, quietly reading beside the lake were much more desirable. That feeling of simplicity and contentment is my motivation for hiking, but that still image isn't as vicariously engaging as the moving image of my tumble, hang and slide. There's no suspense or drama watching someone sit for hours, no matter how blissful they are. Hours of peaceful walking were what I wanted and enjoyed. At the start I knew that was what I wanted, but I also felt compelled that to come back with stories. Stories were what I should have. Relaxation was what I wanted. Walking across Scotland was what I enjoyed. I'd finally arrived at my joy.

Stonehaven started as miles away, but those miles passed easily with no sense of time. Highway signs reminded me that I was getting closer. Eventually I stood at a decision. The main road curved around to the left, bypassing the town but possibly leading travelers to services. Walking straight ahead though, as the original road probably did, steered me into what looked like a fringe neighborhood, possibly a contorted route, possibly leading into an old town center that sustained established establishments. I had my choice of conventions, the new or the old, but no guarantee that either had what I needed. The old road had a sidewalk and more opportunities to ask for directions, so I steered straight and let the modern world swing itself around the town.

The transition to civilization occurred at the border of a plowed field. The British Isles lost most of their trees decades ago for sailing timbers and fuel, but on the other side of the field stood a forest. It was a park and therefore protected. I wondered what monarch preserved that plot. Boisterous hoodlums, really just loud kids, were a shock after hours of solitary quiet. As they came up from behind I shrank from them like a recluse on a rare visit to the city. They dropped over the guardrail and down into a ravine, probably their own private protected plot where they were monarchs in their own realm.

The sidewalk was a welcome relief after shoulder hopping. I followed the road downhill, comfortable with the fact that downhill eventually led to the sea.

I'd been walking so long that I forgot that it was Sunday. When I finally turned the corner into the downtown area I found most of the shops were closed, including the tourist information station. Despite that, Stonehaven was big enough to have everything I needed, including a rail station.

In a shocking change from my rut I found a restaurant where I could actually sit and enjoy lunch. My exuberance entertained the young waitresses whenever they came by my table. I was talkative and happy. Or, maybe they smiled because I looked silly. It took me half of lunch before I realized that the window at the far end of the restaurant had a great view of the water. I saw surf from where I sat. Dean Martin sang in the background. The ubiquitous brown sauce packets caught my eye while I waited for my meal. What was brown sauce? I'd seen it everyday, but it finally struck me how odd it was. What flavor was brown? What ingredient was brown? That was an unpleasant thought. I was easily distracted because sitting down to lunch had become so uncommon. No wonder kids have a rough time sitting still.

Only move when it was to my advantage. Maybe sitting still for the rest of the day was a good idea. The northeast coast was delivering the kind of towns that I could imagine lounging in for days. That may have been true on the west coast, but I was too internally distracted to notice. The water was nearby. I could even catch a train into Glasgow or Edinburgh. That was true for most towns along the line, but the thought seemed more reasonable when I considered it from such an appealing place.

I sat down before noon. Most days I'd walked thirteen miles without a lunch and would run out of energy about 2PM. I gave up on the idea of reaching Aberdeen, but if lunch could sustain me for a few more miles I might be able to reach the next dot on the map, Portlethen. After that, reaching Aberdeen would be an easy half-day walk. I decided to test the power of fish and chips and tea.

The highway grew. South of Stonehaven I'd traveled on one highway. North of town, it swept around and joined up with another larger highway. My route became busier, noisier, and more constant.

My meditations were chopped into shorter segments as I frequently glanced back to check for upcoming hazards. I also glanced away from the highway. That view was as good as ever, whether it was coastline, empty fields, or pastures; but, the highway noise was harder to ignore.

The highway, the railroad, and the coastline closed the gaps between each other. I felt funneled towards a common goal and destination. The cars had an urgency that suggested the drivers were passing through land without noticing it. They got into their boxes in one city, would rumble along for a while, and would only notice the world when their box entered another city. Thousands of people swept by but I had the world to myself as usual.

Fish and chips and tea weren't as powerful as I'd hoped. My legs told me that the afternoon had gone on long enough. Long stretches of empty road were contemplative, but eventually I began contemplating the location of the night's bed. Happily, I found a sign pointing to a hotel. As long as it had rooms and food I'd pay for them, within reason of course. The good news was that the next sign said the turn was in 400 yards. The bad news was that the hotel was four miles up the road after the turn. The land rolled through slight grades that shortened the distance to the horizons. Clusters of home suggested possible places for B&Bs and pubs that were far closer than four miles. Rural was being interrupted by residential. I aimed myself past a few shorter fields and at the houses on the hill.

At the crest was a neighborhood of modest homes with people in the yards. It was rare to find people outside. Almost every house in Scotland appeared vacant or cloistered. Finally, when I needed some help, I found people again. It was probably because it was Sunday. Rumor had it that once upon a time a house at the end of the street had taken in boarders. Maybe they still did. Why not a house closer to the intersection? But I found nothing except more houses. When I finally had enough of hunting for signs that didn't exist I turned around to walk back to the highway. As I did, one gentleman came out of his garage and asked if he could help. I told him my story, He told me that there wasn't a place to stay for miles. I shrugged and sighed, then I thanked him and walked away.

Detours late in the day are never easy because there's less energy left in the body and each step uses a greater fraction of what remains. I hoped his estimate of miles to go was wrong.

I tended to walk the way I was supposed to, facing traffic, which meant that when he drove up less than a mile later I was on the other side of the four lane, median and fence divided highway. He stopped in a narrow and dangerous section and frantically waved me over. Pantomimes didn't dissuade him. I didn't want to cross lanes of busy traffic, but it looked like he was thinking less of his own safety the longer I waited. I jumped the barriers and scurried over to him. He repeatedly told me to get in, get in, as if the cops or some villains were after me. He wanted to drive me to somewhere. He couldn't listen to or understand my logic. Yes, I was tired; but no, I wasn't going to get in a car unless I absolutely had to. I hadn't been in a car, bus, train for weeks. I wasn't going to give up this close to Aberdeen. He would've argued all day. I guess it is part of the way of the world, temptation must be provided as a goal is reached. I seem to recall something similar in Greek mythology, the Bible, and Buddhism. I settled the argument by walking back across the lanes and barriers. I knew what I wanted to do, and I didn't have to win the argument to do it. I was probably impolite and he probably didn't understand this crazy American, but his acceptance was not required. He'd done his duty. The thought was appreciated though.

I could tell I was approaching urban life because a larger patch of suburbia happened soon. As I stepped away from the highway I met a sincerely helpful couple with a kid. Yes, there may be a B&B about a half mile into the neighborhood but they thought the owner might have closed the business. But they were certain that there was a brand new hotel about three miles up the highway. Three miles up the highway sounded like the interminable two miles farther that led me into Glasgow, but it sounded better than yet another dead-end detour. We compared notes on the tiring aspects of the deadweight on my shoulders and the live weight on his. His son wiggled and giggled, which didn't help his Dad's back but was good for our moods.

It was time to tap into my reserves so I could hike three miles, take the crossover, and look down the embankment to the new hotel that was considered too modern, corporate, industrial, and dull. Those were my directions. As I learned, ask three times if you can. A while later I met a very energetic walker that barely stopped as he confirmed the directions. His muscles never relaxed and he sprung off again while I thanked him. He had a lot of pent-up workplace anger and anxiety to release through his heels.

The directions were for three miles. It felt like five miles. It was probably less than one. There was a crossover and a sign welcoming me to Portlethen. The directions steered me to the more vacant side of the highway and a new hotel. I don't know if I would've seen it without their help. I was tired enough to miss signs on towers. I was more likely to watch my feet than the sky.

I was also tired enough that I didn't even want to walk around the shrubbery to the far end of the parking lot and then back to the lobby. I envisioned cutting a straight line through the bushes, exiting with scratches, and then trying to get a room. Walking a few hundred extra feet was better than upsetting the very people that I wanted to get good service from. I tediously took the long route around the parking lot. Yes, they had rooms. Yes, it was the same chain as in Dundee, but this time the rate was 56 pounds. I hoped the restaurant would be better. I knew the view would be the same. Parking lots don't change much. I was definitely glad to be there. She confirmed that I'd walked about 18 miles, possibly my longest day of the trip. If I could trust the maps, I was less than ten miles from my goal of Aberdeen. Hello bed. Hello shower. Hello nap. Where's my dinner? I want a drink.

Dinner was more American than Scottish. The hotel restaurant had a family and businessman design. Everything was new. The menus were laminated. The tables and chairs were designed to be easily cleaned. Ordering was a process instead of a service. I was told to order at the bar and to remember my assigned table number. It was probably an efficient process designed to operate with a high turnover in the wait staff. I followed orders like a worker on an assembly line. A general hum was punctuated by babies crying and children chattering. They gave the room life and energy. Solitary business travelers concentrated on their meals and papers. I wrote and watched the two worlds swirl around each other. My meal must have been well-designed to not offend because it left no impression. I retreated to my room after checking some route details with the front desk and quickly fell asleep.

Tomorrow, my goal, Aberdeen.

Goal!

October 11
Portlethen - Aberdeen

Sleeping in would be a should. I wanted to get to Aberdeen and claim my goal complete. It was only a few miles away and wouldn't take very long, but why wait? If it was only 200 yards I still would've gotten up early. A traveler's Christmas present was waiting to be unwrapped.

My breakfast of two eggs and two undercooked slices of bacon was a little light, but common. I'd traveled farther on less. I also expected to find more food as I approached the city. Aberdeen isn't a town or a village like many of the dots I'd bisected. It is the largest city on that bit of Scottish coast. Its sprawl should be greater than most. Surely I'd find food along the way.

I didn't have a lot of time to spare though. My flight home would depart in less than 50 hours. Any celebration would get slipped into the hours between reaching a room in Aberdeen and the train ride to Glasgow. There wasn't a lot of slack in my schedule.

The highway was too busy enough for comfort, so I started the day by crossing it and walking through the neighborhoods instead. I could afford a bit of a detour. Besides, using suburban sidewalks most of the day was appealing. Sidewalks were wonderful after all of my time along the tussocked shoulders. And, despite what people say about suburbia, and it was quieter than the highway and more interesting than yet another field.

It was a good idea, but that bit of Scotland wasn't built that way. The neighborhood quickly proved to be an island along the highway. Within a mile I was back in countryside and apparently heading to a deadend. Luck arrived. A modern stereotypical schoolgirl, pink clothes more shocking than cute, with white earbuds and cords, walked along the road toward me from somewhere amidst the farms. She nicely stopped and unplugged long enough to give me directions. I should go three miles, but I guessed that she meant about three blocks, pass the hay bales, step around them, and follow the road they blocked. It led to a gap and a gate in the highway fence. I hoped the farmer that planted those bales wouldn't mind a walker strolling by.

A short while later I was walking past a working farm. I didn't notice what was in the rest of the fields because I was distracted by a man and his dog. The man was focused and engaged in his work. I was inconsequential. He'd seen pedestrians before. He was busy reaching into the bed of his pickup, unloading it for the day's chores. His dog was focused and engaged in his work. too. He was statue still, staring at the field. Herding sheep was on his to-do list. They were on the far side of the pasture. He took up a position at the tail end of the truck, slightly crouched, eyes steady on the herd, unmoving while the farmer banged around the back of the pickup finding the right tools for the chores. The farmer put the tools under his arm and clapped a command. The dog was at full speed within a few strides. Some old bit of Greek wisdom came to mind, though I never remember the exact quote. A full life is lived by exercising your skills and talents, on tasks that are interesting and useful, with results that are appreciated and compensated. A dog herded sheep, and looked like it had a full life.

A few hundred feet later was a low wall of hay bales being used more as a barrier than as food storage. Stepping around it wasn't graceful because of some uneven terrain and some trash, but soon enough I was back beside the highway. Just like back in Glasgow, the best directions came from young women who appeared at just the right time. I guess angels can do that. At least this time I remembered the directions.

I wondered if the shortcut would work. I didn't want to get to the highway and find a "Danger, Do Not Enter" sign, or "Keep Out", or absolutely no shoulder. I was relieved. The gap in the fence looked intentional. Plenty of footsteps had stamped a path into the shoulder. If I was doing anything improper, I wasn't the first.

I was back on the highway, which at least would get me to my goal, but the heavy rush hour traffic was hard to ignore. The city was obviously close.

Rural began to lose to intrusions of industrial. Metal buildings were close to the road, and housed people and machines instead of chickens or hay. Acreage turned from green pastures with scattered livestock to grey asphalt with geometric arrays of cars, trucks and boxes. I prefer the green, but I don't mind walking along the grey. They are both realities. Seeing a manufacturing building can be as interesting as seeing a farmer's field, because they both tell stories about people. Guidebooks don't cover the things that fascinate me. I'd rather be open to experience, than be coached on what to witness. It is more fun exercising my senses.

It's hard to miss hitting a city as big as Aberdeen. Eventually I'd find a Welcome sign. I expected that getting directions to my finish line would be tougher. Trial and error could work. So could asking lots of people for directions. Luckily, I found a road crew picking up trash. I approached cautiously because there was the possibility that I shouldn't be walking along the highway, and that they'd enforce that by telling me to leave. None of the rare police cars had stopped or even slowed, but maybe that only meant I wasn't worth their time. It is amazing how much trouble a person can get into by asking simple questions instead of quietly walking by. My good luck continued. One of the crew took the time to give me directions that he assured me would save me a lot of extra walking. The main highway was about to swing around the city, so I should take the spur that peeled off to the right. It's the football route, a term which made more sense to him than me, but that I assumed aimed me towards a stadium. The relief at not being kicked off the highway was enough that I didn't ask for details. He'd already given me more than I could use, mostly about how bad the traffic is on game days and where to go for lunch. A while later I found the turn and took it, and knew that I'd simply keep asking others as I got closer. Besides, if I only followed his directions, I'd end up at the stadium, not the station.

Rural and industrial don't claim every bit of land. Bits of nature utilize every bit of free space and I watch for them. A pond passed by that was fringed with foliage and populated by swans. Fish strike at flies, both natural and artificial. I wasn't the only one that found it. Anglers on one side and swans on the other fed off what they found in the middle. A photograph makes the pond look pristine and something that could be placed in any wilderness, but slightly outside the frame were discarded oil drums, probably empty and rusting back into nature naturally. Nature would win, but it would temporarily be besmirched in the process.

Trail signs pointed me away from the highway, but I wouldn't follow them unless they had a train station symbol and mileage callouts. I'd learned not to trust them. Trail signs that are only directional are useless to people unfamiliar with the trail. Thanks for the suggestion of a direction, and a journey without a goal can be life-changing, but I had a goal and I wanted to reach it. Following someone else's trail simply because it was a trail would take me to their goal, not necessarily mine. A small detour was fine but aimless wandering was only going to happen if I had unlimited time and money. Maybe the universe wants us to float along without a direction, but I wasn't going to trust that on the last day with less than 48 hours until my flight. I wanted a reason for celebration, not consternation. I wanted to finish my trip with joy.

A highway sign welcomed me to Aberdeen, but it didn't have the same effect as encountering neighborhoods, bus stops, pipelines, and rail lines. It was just the massive metal highway sign that was on the other side of the highway. Anywhere I stopped I could claim to have made it to Aberdeen. A taxi, a train, and a plane could get me home, but I wouldn't feel satisfied until I walked into a hotel or the Aberdeen train station. I had enough for bragging rights, but they didn't interest me as much anymore.

I thought that I'd feel greater relief with each step. Internally I had expectations of emotions and thoughts as if there was a script for what I'd just accomplished, but it wasn't being played out. I'd reached my goal. Every extra step was a bonus. But, maybe I'd kept something locked down and the relief triggered a release again, just like in Glenfarg. Maybe I just had a random bit of bad day show up that would've been there even if I hadn't just crossed a finish line. An anxiety attack hit as I walked past car lots and strip malls. My chest tightened. My mood crashed. It felt like a reprise of the climb out of Cairnryan on the first day, but this time the land was flat and I was amidst civilization. If I collapsed it would be within sight of hundreds. Help would come quickly with flashing lights and a short drive to a hospital. My celebratory mood was set aside. I stopped. I took deep breaths. I grabbed my water bottle and drank, hoping my condition was merely dehydration. I wasn't cramping, but habits from my running days convinced me to find a banana as a source of potassium. There was no reason to believe that potassium deficiency was the problem, but it was an action I could take that had no downside. I was determined to walk on, and so I did. If I collapsed I wanted it to be at the downtown train station, ticket to Glasgow in hand.

It was frustrating and maddening to have a complete reversal from what I expected. My steps should've been lighter. My strides longer and more relaxed. My head up and a smile on my face. But I grimaced from a pain that had no obvious source. It felt like a deity decided to remind me how much I hurt at the start, so I'd have a fresh contrast with the celebration. I thought I might die. I didn't care how important the lesson might be, I didn't like the class or the training or the testing I was going through. I vented, fought the feeling, and just kept walking.

In less than a mile my mood began to improve. The railroad arrived. Granted, it was on the other side of the river, but a short while later I found a bridge that took me to the other side. I left the gloom behind. Follow the railroad and find the train station. Unambiguous logic. I loved it.

Architecture aged as I got closer to the city center. Strip malls were replaced with shops built into arches beneath the rails. Buildings were closer to the point that the railroad ran overhead instead of across open land. I was glad to find the railroad, but had no idea which side of it I should follow to get to the station. Picking the wrong side could be a long detour. A businessman gave me directions to go through an underpass and then follow the road as it climbed back above the rails. According to him I couldn't miss the station. He didn't know me very well. His directions sounded too concise and the distance too close. He hadn't told me, "just two more miles."

The short climb delivered an ache to my legs, which made me realize that the other pains were gone. Aches in one part of my body had become opportunities to notice how well the rest felt. My back, shoulders, feet, and mood had recovered. Some light huffing and puffing brought me to the level of the railroad, and then above it. At the next intersection was an overpass. I crossed it halfway, stood in the middle, and looked down on the tracks of Aberdeen's train station. I'd made it! Standing above the station felt like standing atop a peak: tired, jubilant and proud - looking forward to rest, food and drink. I would've patted myself on the back, but I was wearing my pack. I'd done it. I'd crossed Scotland on foot, no cars, buses, or trains. From the Irish Sea to the North Sea. Through every shade of rural and urban. Under grey skies and blue. Meeting an introverted group of extroverts who were better at expressing themselves than I was. I'd seen a slice of the country that didn't fit in anyone else's book. And I had Guinness almost every night.

Now, where was some food and something to drink? But first, where was the front door to the station? Where was my finish line?

I couldn't find the station. I'd seen one side of the tracks. I crossed to the other side and only found a city and a shopping mall. For all I knew, the rails went into some tunnel. They do that in Seattle. Maybe the station was really on the other side of the city. How could I follow them? Oh no. Had I celebrated too soon? Hubris tastes bitter. When in doubt, follow the flow. Cross the bridge over the tracks and follow the folks into the mall. Maybe I could find directions there. And there it was. Off to the side was the ticket counter and the entrance to the station. Hallelujah!

No brass band played. No banners were strung up. To everyone there I was another person to ignore as they went about their day. We rarely know the stories that pass by in the strangers we see. They probably had good stories too. Maybe there should always be a brass band, or bagpipes considering where I was. Every day there are reasons to celebrate.

My celebration would happen. It was a matter of time, but while I was there I decided to check out the train schedule. The ticket line was nearly vacant. The attendant verified that there'd be a train to Glasgow the next day because there were several trains a day. I'd forgotten my experience at the Glasgow station. Of course, there'd be a train. I could get a reservation, but there probably wasn't a need on the post-rush hour train. By the way, I could save 25 pounds by buying my ticket a day early. I still had a return ticket from when I traveled from Glasgow to Stranraer. Could that be used as a credit? I'd kept it because they didn't sell one-way tickets, and because it was a comfort sitting in my wallet if I wanted a quick trip back. The ticket was out of date, but at least it was worth a laugh. He pointed out that it was for seniors. The young pup in Glasgow thought I was much older than I was. The ticket agent in Aberdeen saw me as middle-aged. Maybe the walk rejuvenated me.

There was a big Jury's Inn sign on the side of the building, another in the chain that I'd used in Glasgow. I couldn't find their front door either. Evidently it was in the mall somewhere. I walked back in and couldn't find a sign or help from a mall map. Back outside, across the street from the modern mall was a proper old hotel with a recognizable front door. Thank you for simplicity.

They had rooms, but they weren't ready yet. I arrived too soon. It had been a busy morning for me. They suggested and I agreed that an early Guinness and lunch were a good idea.

After checking in, I happily took the elevator instead of the elegant old staircase, found my room, and collapsed into a nap. As I lay down, the sun came out, brightened the room, and matched my mood.

If I had a travel partner, I'd probably would've devoted the afternoon to sitting and sipping and sharing. Laughing would've been involved. The closest I could get to my friends was via computer. A classic old hotel didn't have a modern computer for its guests, but they knew I could find one over at the main library. It was a short walk that took me past traditional massive stone architecture, or at least it felt that way to a person who lives amongst buildings that are all less than a hundred years old and that are usually made of wood. The sun was shining on a park. People were walking around during their lunch hour. I was in a city and an environment radically different than my normal days for almost a month. I felt like a traveler and a tourist again. There was no pack on my back, the weather was fine, and I could stroll, stop, amble, peruse, do anything I wanted because I'd reached my destination.

The library was a marvelous and a fine place to linger, but I was there for a short purpose. A lot of floor space had been redesigned to accommodate computers and their users. That was welcoming to me, but probably not to the displaced books. Getting a visitor's account was a bit more of a hassle than in the smaller libraries, but that wasn't a surprise. They gave me a short time limit, so I didn't get everything done; but, I did enough to share my accomplishment.

I wandered a bit more through the local streets. It was different not having a goal and not having to worry about where to eat and sleep. Twenty days had ingrained a new set of habits, which was one of the goals. The contrast gave me a new perspective on my normal life. I was sure that would manifest itself and persist over months, hopefully years. My bicycle ride across America continued to reveal insights more than a decade later. Walking across Scotland would probably do the same.

I'd already seen the innovative mall and station combination, the classic hotel, and the venerable public buildings. My afternoon sojourn gave me a broader picture of Aberdeen because it took me past some questionable businesses that looked like they thrived thanks to sailors. I didn't try window shopping there. The better entertainment was an outdoor musician wearing a kilt and playing bagpipes. In weeks in Scotland, he was the first man I'd seen in a kilt, and the first bagpipe I'd heard. I'd seen plenty of kilt shops, but that's like saying I've seen plenty of tuxedo shops back home. It doesn't mean I see many men in tuxedos. An afternoon spent at an ambling pace was hours spent relaxing without worry.

People watching is always great entertainment. There was a great contrast, not Scotland versus America, but rural versus urban. City shoes are built for pavement and carpets. How do women walk that way? My hiking boots were obviously out of place in shopping malls and hotel lobbies. Clomping across the lobby in Glasgow was noisy proof. A farmer from Scotland may be more comfortable on a farm in America. Mud boots work the same in both places. In my opinion, if an American wants a different cultural experience there's no reason to cross a border. Someone from New York City could have a harder time adjusting to a small town in West Virginia than they could adjusting to downtown Glasgow. Someone from Aberdeen might not know what to do in the Highlands. Some folks from the small towns I visited would probably look out of place as they came out of the train station.

I knew I was a tourist because I didn't fit in, but I was comfortable because I'd become more comfortable with myself. I was wore what I carried. I was my own fashion statement based on my values, needs, and resources. Whether I stood out or fit in didn't matter. Three weeks at the beach wouldn't have produced the same change. Three weeks of introspection capped with an accomplishment was much more gratifying and liberating.

Dinner was sedate. Celebrating alone is a quiet thing. Standing up and dancing around the dining room would be more than a bit out of place. Besides, there was no one to dance with. The restaurant was filled with quiet businessmen and loud sailors. Any woman was most likely to be part of the wait staff. I ate red meat to celebrate, but also to fill any deficiency. I hadn't forgotten that mood crash from earlier in the day. I never drank so much Guinness, except back in college, and I finished it off with a ritual whisky.

I was glad for my notepad dinner companion. Writing was better than the lonely looks of the solitary men staring at their plates or empty tables. It would've been odd to stare at the distracting sailors.

My notes weren't just a distraction. They were entertaining. Places blur. Memories easily intermingle, switch order, revise weather, selectively forget odd moments. I looked back and quickly replayed the walk. My memory already had confused details and forgotten some episodes, and that had nothing to do with the whisky dessert. No wonder human communication is so difficult. My memories didn't agree with my observations. Add another person and there are an infinity of possible misinterpretations.

The next day's train ride would replay two-thirds of the walk within a few hours. It would be an interesting double check against my notes.

I hadn't followed a sightseer's tour. Sightseers see clusters of sights and focus on places with lots of signage, services and explanations. What I saw was a lot of world that I interpreted my way. People are concentrated in cities, but cities aren't very wide. Every city could've been crossed in less than a day. The majority of my time was spent in the rest of the world, which isn't wild, but is much quieter. I'd seen cities by bisecting them, seeing a few of the sights, and seeing even more of how people live, whether they struggle or indulge. I'd followed my own path, which may not make sense to many or any of them. I'd walked across a country that is encouraging people to walk, but only walked with a member of a road crew, a recently divorced extrovert, a businessman, and a litter-picker. The total time spent with them was less than an hour. I was in cloistered meditation for three weeks.

My estimate of the total distance was just shy of 250 miles, probably 247 miles. I'd averaged 13 miles a day, walking a half-marathon that took much longer than my running times. The train ride would rewind more than a week of travel in less than half a day. It would see the same terrain, but it wouldn't be the same experience. I could only get there by being there and seeing it as a here, at my pace, following my path. The journey was the goal, and the journey isn't just the line on the map, but how that line is followed. Someone else walking the same line would have a different journey and reach a different goal even if they arrived at the same place in the same amount of time. By walking my way, I found a hint of the joy that resides within every moment. I found that I'd lived decades of service and responsibility and denial thinking that giving of myself would help me find that joy. That was right and wrong.

I learned that I could find that joy anytime, anywhere; but, doing that easily would take practice. That joy is there, and always was, even if I forgot to look for it. It exists here and now and I wonder if most people have a tougher time finding it than I do. There's enough anger and angst in the world that I suspect that many people are far from joy. I find that joy more readily now, and am learning to live closer to it. But I also realized that for decades I denied joy because it was possibly self-indulgent, that it was possibly disrespecting others. I'd gone too far and disrespected myself. My active denial created a rut of habits that were deep. I could pull myself out of with effort and slip back in too easily. Living with joy would require practice. For many, there's a nobility in suffering, and a dismissal of those who find silver linings. They may have gone too far, may be flipped the wrong way, but I could step past that perspective, view and horizon and flip my world back my way.

Few would see the rowdy sailors as role models, but I enjoyed their exuberance. I couldn't tell if their noise level measured their joy level, but I was happy to see them as uninhibited; especially, in contrast to the dour businessmen. Neither group knew what level of anxiety, determination, celebration, and joy I'd felt within the past 24 hours. That's true of anyone. That's even true of friends if conversations are defined by what they avoid instead of what they include. We can't see inside each other's heads. But the effort is appreciated.

Philosophical considerations aside, I finished my whisky by toasting myself, and then I went upstairs for the night.

My finances weren't affected by my joy. The objective and the subjective were not synchronized. The stock market had not been kind to my portfolio while I was gone. I felt the pinch. I could spend a day playing tourist in Glasgow, which felt like a should, or I could head straight to the airport and try to fly home a day early. The price of shifting my ticket might be much less than another night in Glasgow. The amount I saved could fund a celebration at home, and I missed my home. Three weeks was long enough.

In all the time in Scotland I'd never found a shepherd's pie. That struck me more than possibly missing a sightseeing tour. Well, at least I knew what I wanted.

Replay

October 12
Aberdeen - Glasgow

Sleeping in took effort. Waking up early had become my new habit. I had to remind myself that I didn't have anywhere to go or anything to do until I caught the 10:38 to Glasgow. I snuggled back under the covers for a while, but it didn't last. Since I'd finished I was famished. Every meal wasn't big enough and I wasn't going to miss breakfast.

I opened the window and smelled the early morning urban aroma. That wasn't a good idea. Evidently during the night someone used the sidewalk for a urinal. Herds of livestock working constantly didn't create such an unappealing odor. Even the

manure spreaders didn't compare. I closed the
window and appreciated the small towns I'd stayed in.

After checking out I wandered around the city
for a while. Most of the stores were closed. The
sidewalks were busy with people heading to work.
Eventually I wandered back towards the station. I
didn't want to miss my train. I spent some time
walking through the mall and was surprised to find a
theater. I could've watched a movie after dinner
instead of retreating to my room. It would be
interesting to see if Scottish crowds were more polite
than the folks in the mall theaters back home. Are cell
phones really that necessary? The movies looked the
same. Hollywood has reach.

I should've bought a reserved seat. Yes, it was
the post-rush hour train, and yes, it normally would
be empty; but, for once it was nearly completely
booked. Almost every seat had a Reserved tag. I'd
hoped for a forward facing seat on the sea side so I
could watch the route rewind and relax. I skipped the
first few open seats so I could get the best view and
ride, but soon every seat had a "Reserved" sign on it.
The next two cars were booked. The only seat I found
was a foldout seat on the land side looking back. It
was better than standing the entire way from
Aberdeen to Glasgow. Of course, I stood the entire
way from Glasgow to Aberdeen, but that was while I
was walking.

The ticket seller would normally have been
right about the train being empty, but this was a rare
occasion. Some major tournament was being played
in Glasgow and teams from throughout Scotland were
congregating. Teams traveled as a team, everyone
organized and everyone wearing the same uniform.
They weren't wearing their playing uniforms of shorts

and shirts. They showed team solidarity by wearing the same traveling uniform: tartaned kilts. The train was populated with a couple of hundred men in proud plaid. They enjoyed traveling together, especially after the beer trolley came down the aisle. Hundreds of men drinking beers before lunch. They played cribbage. They sang. They laughed. A few read.

Then, at about the same time, they stood in a very long line. The beer made its way through them and needed to be released. The train had two toilets. One plugged almost immediately. The other was beside my seat. For the next few hours I sat beside a line of hairy legs that were jostled as the train rolled along. It was not the view I hoped for. Despite the inconvenience, and maybe because of the beer, they were generally a happy bunch. The rest of the passengers avoided eye contact, but the players were amongst friends. They were even nice enough to let a mother with child walk to the front of the line. Very considerate. Very gentlemanly. Weeks in Scotland and I hadn't seen my first kilt until the day I entered Aberdeen. Then I was inundated with them in close proximity for hours.

The train's route roughly followed mine, but the routes were different enough, and my seat was pointed in the wrong direction, so I rarely caught reminiscent glimpses of where I'd been. I'd have to rely on my notes, my photos, and my memories. My ride passed in crowded solitude while I watched unfamiliar territory.

Reaching Glasgow station was a relief in many ways. Glasgow smelled fresh and clean, and it wasn't raining! Serendipity happens. As I stepped out of Glasgow station I found myself at the airporter bus which was ready to go. I can take a hint and got on. I guessed I'd try to catch an early flight and save some money. I'd miss my only day of sightseeing, but I was ready to be home.

Maybe serendipity simply wanted me out of the city. There was no early flight. The next flight out was the one on my ticket for the next day. It was late afternoon and I had almost 24 hours before check-in. That's a lot of time to spend in an airport. Oh well, it wouldn't be optimum, but I decided to get a room by the airport and get horizontal for a while. It was probably cheaper than staying downtown anyway. I ambled over to the tourist information booth that helped me get everything started weeks earlier. It would've been nice to visit with the man who helped me, but he was out. Instead I got the news that the teams had booked every room throughout Glasgow and even around the airport. It was a good thing that I hadn't tried for a room in the middle of the city. My day in Glasgow would've turned into hours of hotel shopping. The term "hundreds of pounds" came up when I asked for the price of any remaining room. The only place I could stay was in the airport waiting area - for over twenty hours. Walking was much more empowering than waiting, but there was nowhere to walk that wasn't just pacing and nowhere to sleep that wasn't uncomfortable. Reservations and itineraries do have their benefits.

I spent the next few hours alternating between eating, drinking, walking, napping, and regularly calling the same hotels for cancellations. One hotel was close enough that I walked over to their lobby instead of listening to voice menus. As I stood in line I wanted to jump at an American who dismissed a room because it was a smoking room. I wasn't so picky. I could spent the night in the airport, but that would put an uncomfortable end to an enlightening trip. The room was taken by the time I got to the head of the line. I walked back to the airport and started the cycle again.

I'd become accustomed to quiet inns, quiet days, quiet people, with the ambience of some laughs thrown in. I was back in an urban freneticism. American accents carried, but I probably noticed them more because I hadn't heard an American in weeks except on TV. Some people spoke so loudly that I wondered about their hearing until I noticed that they understood quiet voices too. Then I realized that they weren't aware of how loud they were because they weren't listening to anyone, including themself. They were making noise because that's what they thought people did. I wondered if they ever quietly sat, and whether that would scare them.

My silly persistence paid off. At 6PM, about 15 hours before my flight so more like 12 hours before I had to check out, I found a room for 100 pounds. It was within walking distance, even for people who didn't walk across Scotland. I didn't wait for a taxi or bus. I got directions and walked quickly, only making one wrong turn, to check into the highest tech room of the trip. I ordered room service so I wouldn't have to spend time waiting for a waiter, and then jumped into a quick modern shower. The rest of my time was spent catching up on the world via the in-room computer simply because I could, and then relaxed into the night. My back definitely approved of the choice of hotel bed over airport bench. Comfort was a celebration.

Rewind

October 13, Glasgow - Seattle

I paid a lot for a room that I wasn't in long, and I still got up before the alarm. I didn't want to miss my 9AM flight. My schedule was no longer defined by me, but luckily it fit the schedule I'd followed for weeks. Breakfast was quick, and possibly underdone. I didn't even wait for the shuttle. Trying to rewind my walk to the airport I managed to get lost only once again, and got there about the same time as the shuttle. At least I got some exercise. There would be very few chances for aerobics in the hours of flights to Seattle.

Airport security ramped up because of a terror alert. My water bottle bought in the Glasgow airport wasn't allowed to pass through Heathrow. They took it away after offering me a drink from it. I was 50 pence shy of replacing it. At least I wasn't carrying a lot of foreign currency that would be useless at home. Unfortunately, it looked like I might be dehydrated by the time I got there. Security at each airport escalated until an anxiety attack threatened to flare up. I barely made my last flight because I was directed through an extra security checkpoint. My route across the pasture above Cairnryan and the farmyard outside Girvan meant that me, my pack, and especially my boots were screened for anything that might pass along

Hoof and Mouth or Mad Cow disease. For three
flights I went through six security checkpoints. My
three flights: from Glasgow to Heathrow to
Philadelphia to Seattle required ten flight numbers.
Every flight was packed enough to only allow
elbowroom on one. The rest of the time was the now-
familiar press of humanity, the new jet age.

Three weeks of unwinding were countered by
hours of waiting in lines as clocks ticked and
airplanes prepared for departures. My anxieties only
began to subside when I boarded the flight to Seattle.
My back was twitchy from trying to conform to the
seats. The rest of me was going through the culture
shock of rejoining the mainstream. Fitting back
within its borders required an effort. Please remain
seated. Your dinner choices are chicken or pasta.
Secure your tray table. Have a nice day. Maybe my
muscles were twitching because they were trying to
walk while being forced to sit. They weren't used to
conforming to a sedentary existence.

My mind had fewer constraints. It was full of
impressions, memories, and images that were more
interesting than the movie or a nap. I wrote a few
notes, but I knew they were catchphrases. A larger
and deeper story was developing within my
subconscious. The back of my brain was busy. The
longer story had to simmer down to a reduced
essence, and there was no reason to rush it. I looked
forward to my dreams, where my subconscious could
use much more than words to tell me my own story. I
didn't want to distract it, but my brain did start ticking
through possible titles. Despite my original intention,
my vacation was evidently going to become a book.
Who made that decision? At least I listened to my
intuition.

As I sat there wedged into a safe seat, I noticed which moments were easiest to remember. They were a mix. The heart attack hill in Cairnryan and the view from the top. The sunset in Prestwick. The eternal two more miles into Glasgow. Walking the Kirkintilloch canals lined with autumn colors, ending at Denny. The manifested B&B in Fossoway. The beautiful foggy day outside Arbroath. The guy trying to give me a ride into Aberdeen. The memory that stood above the rest was my stay in Fenwick. The Langside B&B had style, character, and an ambiance that set me up for the next day's revelation.

I experienced a pure moment of joy. I'd felt joy before, but I had never realized that joy was in every moment. Every moment contains every emotion. I merely had to make the choice to feel joy. Fifty years of not being aware of that was startling. It meant I'd missed a lot of joy. I thought joy would arrive because I'd done everything I should do. Within the last few years I thought joy might arrive because I'd done something I'd wanted to do. That day outside of Fenwick taught me that joy didn't have to arrive. Joy was already there, always was, and always would be. I simply had to choose it out of all the possible emotions. I also realized that fifty years of habits may not evaporate with one moment's revelation. I'd have to practice experiencing joy. That one moment was worth putting everything on the credit card. Seeing how close joy is at any moment was a better view of my inner self than any probing diagnostic prescribed by my doctor. Weeks of mining can produce a single nugget worthy of the effort. It didn't ease my back, but it did ease my mind.

After twenty hours I was home. Happiness was catching the early shuttle and getting back home to hot water, a wide bed, and my familiar life.

The trip across Scotland was over. The trip to living my life in joy was just beginning.

Home - Epilogue

Several months passed before I began to write. My subconscious musings delivered the insight that I "should want joy". It would be too easy to treat the insight as an idea or a should. As an idea, "should want joy" was valuable, but it was too easy to make it a philosophical abstraction. Thinking about it wasn't as valuable as doing it and feeling it. Joy is real and doesn't need to be analyzed or debated.

I stepped past horizons every day. Most travelers do. Each day's walk carried me past the morning's view. Sometimes that was as easy as walking around a ridge. A few hours of the simple act of moving my feet carried me to the next town and more beyond. Some people stayed in those towns, within these horizons, for years or decades. They had everything they needed so there was no incentive to look for something different. Why spend money on something that wasn't necessary?

Stepping past my internal and personal horizons was more of an accomplishment than walking to Aberdeen. My goal was external and planned. My accomplishment was internally and unexpected. My most powerful memories weren't of scenes, but of emotions. They weren't about the mileage or the daily goals, but about the lives and nature that I'd passed through. Guinness and whisky are good, and a fine way to celebrate an eighteen mile walk, but if it was only the mileage I could've bought a keg and a cask, had them delivered to my house, and then walked in circles for hours.

Of course, I went to Scotland to have a vacation. Curiosity drives some travelers like me. With a bit of curiosity and a bit of good luck I learned what other worlds, views, and experiences existed. I've seen examples of other life choices. Vacations are sold as exuberance, indulgence, and frivolity. Walking across Scotland was not that kind of vacation. My vacation was an escape from my normal routine that made me aware of what I enjoyed and what I wanted to change. It wasn't dynamic enough for video. My best moments could be captured by a still camera, but the expression or posture wouldn't make sense without a caption. Every day had various degrees of such moments.

Every day also had its own unphilosophical collection of aches, pains, and anxieties. The roster was extensive and they tag teamed each other, always reminding me of mortality or at least age-induced use and vulnerabilities. I lead an active life. My body knows it. We negotiate it daily. Walking an average of a half-marathon each day provided more than the usual number of opportunities for discussion.

For those who want details, I'll at least list: shoulders from carrying the pack, something in the vicinity of my gall bladder, hips and back from uneven surfaces, leg nerves from the hip belt, Achilles' tendon, ball of the left foot from an exacerbated dancing condition, jammed toenails from stopping suddenly, worrisome ankles from shoulder hopping, and a series of pains from a tight and bulky pack strap that caused an upper left chest ache over my heart and a lot of worry. Middle-age and chest pains are a worrisome combination. A long list of aches ignores the fact that the list of what worked would be even longer. It was hard, but helpful, to keep that in mind. The physical problems never showed.

Even amidst my physical symptoms, I knew my mental health was improving when I felt an unexpected laugh, a broader smile, or a quiet pause. At one point I made the transition from considering what others thought of my trip to the fact that I couldn't imagine a better one. Better, I finally internalized, was best measured by my desires. Others thought I should go some place sunny and warm, hang out in the pubs more, hike the ruins or the wildernesses. I realized that I wanted movement more than stillness, quiet more than crowds, and a journey where I set the expectations rather than a tour that could be measured against guidebooks.

Everything I needed for a three week journey fit into my oversized daypack, and those weeks could have been six or thirty or whatever. I also packed fewer worries. I spent a lot less time worrying about my house, car, chores, obligations, and friends. No wonder nomads smile a lot.

I wanted to walk through foreign but familiar surroundings that were pleasant and reasonably safe. I got that. Scotland was a country-sized comfort zone. It took me a while to appreciate it. That's a surprise considering that I was the one who made the choice. My intuition suggested it and I trusted it but without understanding. There was no drama to suggest an excursion beyond my borders, boundaries or world view, but internal growth can be subtle, pervasive, and permanent. Some part of me knew that I was ready for it. I'm glad I listened to me. Evidently, my self knows me well.

The morning walk out of Fenwick was the key. It would become the long, exasperating day of "two more miles" that ended in exhaustion in Glasgow. Who would sign up for something like that? But early in the morning, along a lonely stretch of bike path I had my moment of joy. It wasn't an idyllic setting. The gray skies and isolation weren't extolled and sold in any guidebook. I was simply walking past fields and pastures, wondering again about the cost of the trip. What else could I have done with a few thousand dollars? There were plenty of household repairs to do. Doctors had lots of ideas for diagnostic testing. Hawaii and Vegas sounded much better, but I couldn't get excited about them. Fiscally they may have been better deals, but why weren't they attractive? I didn't want to lounge around all day. My body had already told me that. I didn't want noise and frantic action. What I wanted was to walk quietly. Walking along a lonely path was what I actually wanted to do. The should didn't matter. There was no want because I already had it. Some, most, people learn joy as children. As a child I spent a lot of time doing what I was told, acting as I should, and dismissing what I wanted because good things come to those who wait. I got the impression that if I did everything I was supposed to do, everything I should, that I'd get everything I wanted and that I'd enjoy life. One moment on the outskirts of Fenwick made me smile when I saw how silly that idea was, and made me sigh when I realized how much joy I'd missed in 51 years.

I changed my life by walking across Scotland.

The moment wouldn't show up in a movie. I smiled and sighed. I kept walking. And then it was gone, except for one thread of that feeling that was tied to an anchored memory. I am cautiously reeling in that frail line. The story of the moment is valuable to me and dull for most spectators. "He learned something at 51 that 5 year olds know too well. So what?" Others with similar revelations understand. If it improves the rest of my life, it was worth the money.

For three weeks I got up at around seven, packed, had the same eggs and "bacon" breakfast, followed by hours of non-stop walking, ending at an early check-in, recuperating, a nice dinner, probably a Guinness and maybe a whisky, and an attempt at sleep. At some level my journey was nothing more than one rut replacing another. For me, the best way to understand one rut is to jump into another. I found joy in one and realized it had to be in the other too. A deep enough rut has very near horizons. Stepping from one to the other showed me what was within and outside both; broader horizons and incredible views. By stepping out of my rut I appreciated what I had and saw beyond my horizons.

I spent three weeks walking, thinking, and drinking my way across Scotland. My journey continues. There's a horizon ahead, and I wonder what lies beyond it - and whether I can get a beer and a bed there.

About the author:

I am an odd mix who got this way by following intuition and curiosity. The world draws me along as I seek knowledge and insight. My adult journey started as an engineer at Boeing (aerodynamics, rocket science, that sort of thing), I slid into an, apparently temporary, early retirement (frugality has its benefits and investing has its risks), and now the journey has plopped me into the life of a writer (books of cultural and nature essays: Just Keep Pedaling, Twelve Months at Barclay Lake, Twelve Months at Lake Valhalla, Twelve Months at Merritt Lake, and even one about life and money, Dream. Invest. Live), as a photographer (Twelve Months at Cultus Bay, Penn Cove, Admiralty Head, Deception Pass, and Double Bluff), and as a speaker (I'll talk about any of my books, and also teach classes in Modern Self-Publishing and Social Media). Who knows where it will flow next?

My books and photos are the products of my curiosity and my search for insights into our world, or at least my world. We live in a fascinating place and time; and whether that is for a reason, or just by chance, such a life is amazingly rich with experiences and connections. The best way to feel the sense the world is to be active enough to get out into it, and quiet enough to observe it.

Tom Trimbath

"Culture defines itself by what it maintains meticulously and what it ignores." "Enjoys..."

Tom Trimbath

21673527R00145

Made in the USA
Charleston, SC
26 August 2013